MAKING MILLIONS

How Ordinary Teens Can Transform into
High Earners and How You Can Too

NOTE FROM THE AUTHOR

What's the secret to transforming your earnings in your teens or early twenties? Well, let me tell you what it's not straight off the bat. It's not about having rich parents. Or going to the right school. Or having friends in high places. In fact, you don't need to feel very special or unusual at all. In this book, learn how you can transform your earnings and take control of your life.

In twelve chapters packed with sound business advice, you'll discover a different route to making a living online and offline (with a side-serving of fame, if that's your goal!). You'll follow the stories of successful young business owners, who started out just like you before going on to become stand-out successes in their chosen fields.

Get heaps of practical tips to kickstart your journey in entrepreneurship, eCommerce or social media management. Learn about the gig economy and career surfing, apprenticeships and online courses, discover apps that will help you to network and grow your career and a range of occupations and ways to earn a living that you may never have considered. The insights are simple and many require little or no money to implement, so you can get started right now.

As jobs die on the high street and are reborn online, you need a different set of role models to show you the way. Whether you want to build a brand, achieve financial security or you're just worried about paying your way through college and getting a job afterwards, this book is here to challenge your assumptions about work and empower you to own your future.

ABOUT THE AUTHOR

Fiona, the mother of a teenager, is a business psychologist and linguist with international experience in people development, assessment, psychometric testing, mentoring and coaching. She is the founder of Cosmikos, offering coaching to young adults and parents. She is also a writer and speaker.

TABLE OF CONTENTS

MAKING MILLIONS

ADDENDUM

As I write this addendum to my book, my family and I are in lockdown and have been for six weeks already. You're living this moment in history in a liminal space between what was and what's going to be. Today I attended a webinar, sent flowers to a friend, did two coaching calls and my teen attended lectures, all from the comfort of home. This way of working and playing is not going away. A time of great disruption is often a time of great opportunity but be prepared to pivot in response to what's happening around you. Read articles about the impact of the pandemic on business, society and culture. Scrutinise what's happening in the world around you. If you don't see it, you can't seize it! What are people doing differently? Is it efficient? Could it be improved? Could you save them money? Are there gaps in the market? Joe Wicks spotted a gap in the market for families stuck at home unable to leave the house to exercise. His business saw staggering growth as a result. A time of disruption is also a time to seek out and test new strategies and connect with a network of people interested in the same things as you. Read on to discover how.

MAKING MILLIONS

ACKNOWLEDGEMENTS

I'd like to pay special tribute to the entrepreneurs and influencers whose stories inspired me to write this book. There is invaluable learning in stories and teenagers and graduates need role models their own age, with knowledge and wisdom to share, to identify and relate to jobs as a route to earning money, becoming independent and flourishing creatively. In the interest of full disclosure, I've had the real pleasure of interviewing or communicating directly with half of the young people who feature in the book. However, you will also read accounts of entrepreneurs I haven't interviewed or spoken to, whose stories I've curated and researched from publicly available records with careful reference to sources, namely Rachel Parcell, Holly Hubert, Fleur de Force, Ben Francis, Sean Young, Sara Tasker, Ben Towers and Luka Sabbat. All of the people who feature in the book are exemplary in how they conduct their businesses and live their lives. A huge thank you to everyone involved, including all the school leavers who completed online surveys.

For Sandra Hinshelwood for her invaluable support and considerable network, thank you. With thanks to the Pat Mesiti book team for their guidance and professionalism. For Alexa, Annette, Charlie and Marisa. You know who you are!

For my parents: Mary Bridget (whose love of learning inspired us all) and John Valentine O' Neill in deepest gratitude.

Finally, for Alex. For being an original! It is my joy to spend time on this planet with you.

FOREWORD

I would like to see this book on the bookshelf of every teen and in every school library. It includes the knowledge and wisdom, necessary to pursue a profitable career, that I wish I'd received growing up.

You will discover how teenagers from all walks of life, and with no unfair advantage whatsoever, have become six and seven-figure earners, just by leveraging what they use every day. A computer and an internet connection. It will inspire and motivate you to go ahead and monetise your knowledge and passion the fast and easy way.

Read the book cover to cover, absorb all the gold nuggets shared and make your life a masterpiece.

Steven Essa

6

INTRODUCTION

Kickstarting a career can be challenging. Making the all-important transition between education and work is a step that many of you put off for as long as possible as there is rarely a clear path to follow. This book highlights the huge number of ways to earn a living in the 2020s. It shows you how to take small steps towards becoming work ready, building career blocks like Lego to help meet the demands of an economy that is rapidly changing and creating work opportunities we couldn't have imagined ten years ago. That the education system needs overhauling to meet the demands of the internet economy is not in doubt nor directly a subject for this book, but that moment is not far off. The Pandemic has positively advanced the case for realigning education with the digital economy and the same heroic efforts that gave us the AstraZeneca and Pfizer jabs can now be focused on the problem of the education gap.

Against this backdrop, we see all around us young people who have successfully transitioned into the new workspace. They're blogging or managing social media accounts, doing gigs or rocketing into cool jobs having completed apprenticeships and are generally thriving in the internet economy. These are young, energetic people, your age or not a lot older than you, not different from or more special than you, who not so long ago were in your shoes, kickstarting careers in their teens. It's difficult not to engage with the stories of how they took on the internet economy and challenged assumptions about earning and marketing, stepping up to take responsibility and refusing to let their age hold them back or define what they were capable of.

This book is for you if:

- You don't want to go to college or university but want some pointers about how to make a living and become financially independent.

- You want to earn but also want the flexibility to work the hours you choose, get up whenever you like and go to bed whenever you like, and all without worrying about money.

- You want to monetise your social media accounts.

- You want to go to university but would like to do gigs (piecemeal jobs) to earn money to help pay your fees.

- You want to know more about passive income and having multiple income streams.

- You think that to make it in the world of online business you need to be "special" in some way.

- You understand the need to network and want to make contact with other young people in the same situation as you and find a way to connect with Big Tech companies looking for ambitious young adults.

- You want to set up your own business eventually but want to know how other entrepreneurs went about it.

- You want to learn more about upskilling yourself to adapt to the marketplace.

- You intend to become a doctor or an engineer but want to keep your options open. We all know of young professionals who've worked their career for five years before pivoting into another job. Consider Adam Kay, former doctor, winner of four National Book Awards who wrote a bestselling book "This is Going to Hurt" about his life as a junior doctor and has just released his second book "Kay's Anatomy".

- You've not considered earning money online until now and want to check out your options.

In the following chapters, you'll hear the stories and examine the strategies of young people like yourself, who have pursued their dreams or set out to conquer the world, some who set out to save the world and those who made money inadvertently whilst pursuing their hobbies. All of these young businesspeople have already seen success but are at different stages of their journey. Everyone has to start somewhere. If you're making initial decisions about earning a living and kickstarting your working life, it's helpful to be able to see the journey from the beginning so that it's relatable but also to see that success doesn't happen overnight. You'll meet young businesspeople who are starting out but already stand out in a sea of enterprising young talent, you'll meet young stars of the business world and older businesspeople challenging assumptions about work. Each has their own inspirational story and you will learn something from all of them. They stand out for their willingness to give things a try, their ability to focus single-mindedly on a goal and an acceptance that their initial efforts are good enough, not perfect.

You can no longer expect to have one lifelong career, but offline employment prospects are being replaced by cool, interesting alternative jobs. Today there are fewer traditional work roles and a huge increase in people working independently, earning a living from running businesses or freelancing. **In the 2020s you don't need to work for someone else from 9 to 5 to earn a living.** From politics to business, the channels we spend our time on and that hold our attention are changing. Even the most traditional companies are turning to influencers to advertise products. Social media is central to showcasing brands, uncovering trends, finding audiences and driving traffic to websites. To thrive in this market, you have to change your assumptions about work. You have to step outside your comfort zone. The young people featured in this book, from influencers to entrepreneurs to freelancers, have embraced the new way of working. The book points you towards opportunities to make money, learn skills and offer your skills (whether in teaching, plastering or coding) on work-for-hire platforms. You can earn on the side while you study or make money as you build a business. You can test out new freelancing work and choose your hours. It's perfectly possible to set aside five hours a week and earn £450–550 per month on one piece of freelance work. We'll examine the strategies used very successfully by young people on platforms from eCommerce to podcasting and YouTube to Pinterest to build their businesses as entrepreneurs, influencers or freelancers. You can work for a Big Tech company and simultaneously volunteer your social media skills for your favourite music festival. If corporate life appeals to you to kickstart your working life, don't be afraid to approach companies without a degree if you have a popular blog or a YouTube channel that you monetise. Demonstrating business intellect is a wide field that is no longer confined to graduates. You'll see that **success is not about being fiendishly clever or somehow "special" and more about consistently applying yourself to a project and not becoming distracted by obstacles.**

In a recent industry survey by the Confederation of British Industry, half of employers reported that young people leaving school or university are not work-ready. However, **the tools necessary to kickstart your career and bring you to the attention of big brands are available online for little or no cost;** programmes that teach you how to run an eCommerce business, write content for marketing, create a website and many more. If you master just one skill, you can access an array of ways to earn a living and become financially independent. This book showcases influencers and entrepreneurs but also high-flying apprentices, inventors, professional app developers and businesspeople working the gig economy, switching careers, earning passive income and having multiple income streams. You will find resources highlighting ways to attract the attention of corporates and how to connect with executives in Big Tech and startups, using various apps.

People sometimes confuse influencers with entrepreneurs. An entrepreneur manages and takes on the risk of a business whereas an influencer is someone who inspires or guides the actions of others, effecting change in people's behaviour. Influencers generate conversation, drive engagement and set trends by being early adopters of new products and services. Influencers, with large, passionate communities often pivot or switch into entrepreneurship which is where the lines between influencer and entrepreneur blur. A classic example of this is when Emma Chamberlain, a fashion and lifestyle influencer, launched her first fashion and accessory line in 2018 to her 5m YouTube followers and 5m Instagram followers. The entire collection sold out within two hours proving that successful influencers can become global entrepreneurs.

The global influencer market is worth up to ten billion dollars today. Social media has become a major source of revenue for people. Blogging remains a multi-million-pound business and all the social media platforms are spawning influencers. Undoubtedly there are lots of influencers in the space and the market has certainly been affected by the pandemic, with business operations disrupted and some brands pulling out of sponsorship deals. Yet most influencers have seen a rise in followers as they adapt and put out content to suit what's happening in the world around them. And many organisations that historically have not used influencers are turning to them now that the only business is online business. One thing is certain, influencers with their acute skillsets will find ways to be part of the economy.

<u>A word about university</u>
Both school and university are a means to an end. The transformation is to earn financial freedom to live the life you want. University is a logical choice for certain career paths such as teachers and doctors. If you're undecided whether university is for you, don't underestimate the value of acquiring key skills that you can monetise as a freelancer, turn into a business or use to get a job offer from a multinational. Success is no longer solely confined to those who have aced exams or gone to a great university. **Having a degree in the 2020s is no longer a guarantee of success.**

Knowing how to create a webinar that converts, how to send traffic to your online shop and how to write content that sells are invaluable skills in the 2020s. Ten years ago, achieving top grades in final exams or an honours degree were the sole factors for employers in assessing your suitability for a job. Today, companies like Google, Microsoft, Amazon, Apple and Facebook sit up and take notice if you demonstrate business intellect, have a strong online presence, create an app, write a blog that attracts thousands of followers, invent a life-saving piece of equipment or successfully sell beauty products on

YouTube from the comfort of your home. Your passion and persistence sell you. Customers, followers and employers alike love a young person on a mission with a sense of urgency to their life.

<u>A word about money</u>

THERE'S NO SHAME IN FOCUSING ON MAKING MONEY. It gives you choices and also allows you to do a lot of good things. As an entrepreneur or employee, you'll help grow the economy, you'll pay taxes and frequent nice hotels and coffee shops and give money to charity. Money helps you to have a positive impact on the world. But a quest for money isn't behind everyone's success story. Many of the people in this book are still on top of their game and reaching for new goals, even years after making their first million. They have that sense of urgency that you must have if you're serious about being successful. Intention is everything.

My wish for this book is that it disrupts the narrative about no jobs and no opportunities and interrupts your belief system that everything is outside your control. In each of the chapters you'll identify alternative ways to market yourself and challenge your assumptions

about earning. If you cast the net wide enough on the different ways to earn a living, you can find a job with earning potential that matches your lifestyle and goals. Whether your motivation is to make a million or simply to avoid the humdrum of nine–to–five office work, whether you want to work 70 hours per week on your startup, 40 hours per week working for Big Tech, 15 hours per week freelancing or earn a living taking photos while you travel the world, there is a way to kickstart this journey and take back control.

I wrote this book to:

- **Inspire confidence** that the first step in kickstarting your working in life is within reach, by introducing you to a range of young people, some making a great success of starting out and others who have persevered and gone on to live the dream life.
- **Spark ideas** about entrepreneurship, influencing, freelancing, multiple income streams and passive income by way of providing an overview of the scope for earning a living.
- **Highlight the opportunities** to make a living on your terms, working the hours you can from wherever you want to be.
- **Examine strategies used by successful young people,** the business ideas, the mental attitude, the hard work.

- Share observations about what I see happening around me in the world of work.
- **Take the fear out of bridging the study–work divide.** There is a wealth of resources and lots of people willing to help you on your journey.

2020 has seen a massively accelerated growth in online business as more buyers and business owners enter the market, all of which translates into new, interesting jobs. The internet is open for business... and business is thriving.

CHAPTER 1
BLOGGING

HOW RACHEL PARCELL RUNS THE MILLION DOLLAR FASHION BUSINESS THAT BEGAN LIFE AS A BLOG ABOUT HER DAILY OUTFITS AND ACCESSORIES.

In 2010, a nineteen-year-old girl called Rachel Parcell from Salt Lake City started a blog called Pink Peonies to document the things that she loved, particularly fashion and accessories. Her first outfit post was in September 2012 - Rachel took a photo of herself wearing a stylish outfit, detailing how she put the look together and posted it online to her 200 followers. The daily outfit idea became a regular post and eventually turned into her career. In 2015 Rachel received an all-expenses-paid invitation to attend New York Fashion Week and her business fate was sealed.

https://www.forbes.com/sites/elanagross/2017/11/03/how-the-26-year-old-founder-of-pink-peonies-turned-her-blog-into-a-million-dollar-business/

Today she runs two businesses: the Pink Peonies blog as well as a million-dollar fashion business called Rachel Parcell Inc. and boasts an online Instagram following of one million. She has proven herself to be a business leader and role model for entrepreneurs. To her daily outfit posts, she now offers style advice and home decor insights. She is also a jewellery designer with her own jewellery collection. She receives thousands of dollars to attend business events and has partnered with TRESemmé amongst many brands.

In short, **in the space of nine years, a young girl, unknown and untrained in the world of fashion, blessed with a camera–ready sense of style, became a top–tier fashion blogger earning upwards of \$1 million dollars annually.** Key to Rachel's success in commanding such fees is that she has amassed a huge number of followers via her posts thereby attracting the attention of fashion houses keen to cash in on the marketing and direct sales opportunities provided by access to her followers. I wanted to include Rachel in the book because, **without real–life stories, it's hard to imagine how a young person, barely out of her teens, could drive US\$1m in sales to a luxury department store chain whilst sitting at home writing her blog!** Check Rachel out here: https://rachelparcell.com.

Never underestimate the power of being able to write

well and communicate ideas skilfully and engagingly. **WRITING IS A SUPERPOWER!** If you have the writing superpower and have an opinion you'd like to share or have an idea for a book or a series of articles, read on to discover strategies for getting started and potentially making a living from writing. If you love physics or cooking, reading or running marathons, you can start a blog or a video log writing about what you love as a means to earn a living. The writing process is easier if you write from personal interest.

<u>Creating a blog</u>

If you don't have a blog and want to start one, check out the articles below. A few tips before you begin. Don't waste money creating a website yet. **Post on established platforms first.** You could post long-form content on Facebook to get traction. Alternatively, if your friend has a popular blog you could ask to guest post on their blog. **Tip: Create your blog once you start getting traction posting your content on small publishing sites or on social media**. Check out the following article:
https://www.wpbeginner.com/beginners-guide/how-to-choose-the-best-blogging-platform/.

Choose your topics carefully. Write about what you know, what you're passionate about. It makes life easier! Choose a couple of areas and write consistently around those themes. Start steady and stick to your schedule. Blog on the side until you start to make enough money from it to secure your future. You will get lots of inspired ideas of things to write about from working or studying and having a life away from your writing desk. Work on a designated day (e.g. Sundays) and try to finish a piece of content in each stint.

Creating valuable content is a way to get you noticed.

If by writing, you are solving a problem for someone or entertaining someone, if you're authentic and provide consistent quality content, you will find a tribe of people willing to engage with and listen to you. With engaged, dedicated followers you could be approached by brands interested in an influencer's ability to drive business their way with a glowing reference or a product mention. In this case you would showcase items by writing about them in the blog content or, more traditionally, ads are placed in the header or sidebar. For interest, brands have been known to approach influencers with a wide range of follower count, from nano influencers (1–9k followers) to micro-influencers (10k +) and macro-influencers (100k +) to mega-influencers (1m+).

<u>Getting published</u>

Tim Denning is a master at writing and getting published and offers excellent free and paid-for online training covering everything from how to write a powerful headline and subtitle to structuring the article and tips for getting published (www.timdenning.com).

Susie Moore, writer and author, has compiled a list of publications to approach with written material. The publications are grouped under editorial themes for ease of reference. Check out Susie's advice for writing to earn a living on www.susie-moore.com. Susie offers free and paid-for training so you can make a start without an upfront lump sum. Learn as much as you can from online freebies then when you start to make some money, invest in your education and buy some courses from the coaches that you've come across who offer real value and interest in your development. Sign up on Susie's website for a list of niche publishers to approach from Daily Bustle in the lifestyle niche to Psychology Today for articles in the self-improvement niche to Forbes or Business Insider magazine in the business niche then get published!

In terms of publicising your blog, it's best to identify which platforms your audience is using, like Pinterest, Facebook, Instagram or Tik-Tok, and target them with informative updates about your blog content up to five times per week or more if you enjoy posting! **You are more likely to earn well from publishing articles than writing a lifestyle blog** (although the latter comes with great job satisfaction if writing is your thing). According to Glen Allsopp of ViperChill, "Even if you're reaching 100,000 readers per day, there are far better ways to monetise your audience." The good news is if you produce some kind of digital product like an eBook or a video series that you can sell from your blog then this will increase your income compared to having ads on your site. WordPress is one of the most popular platforms for bloggers as it has easy themes and plugins which could get you started on your writing journey quite quickly.

Making money from writing

- Start small by sending articles to www.medium.com (an online magazine). They will pay you based on audience engagement with your article. They pay very little, but it makes you a paid writer which will help you find further gigs.
- **Many businesses will pay you for**

consultancy work. You write content for them or help them by mapping out content. You could **write a weekly/monthly niche newsletter** for companies keen to outsource marketing, **manage their social media** or **manage their email marketing**. Few businesses have staff with the time to do it. As I said before writing is considered a type of superpower in the industry. Many people don't have the talent to do it. If you do, exploit that. Check out jobs on sites like www.workinstartups.com and approach companies directly.

- **Write a book**. When you develop a following from blogging or writing a book, people will start to come to you with requests to write articles or speak at their events.

- **Do a paid column**. Once you get established, large publications pay good writers to publish exclusively on their website once or twice a month. **Some publications will pay upwards of US$250 or £190 for an article but you will need a portfolio of work** and already be a published writer. Start small with publications that pay less and work your way towards earning the big money.

- **Become a ghost writer**. Katie Price and Rihanna have famously paid others to ghost write their books. If you're happy not to get credit for your writing, this might be a good option. Advertise your services as a ghost writer. Use work-for-hire platforms like Upwork, Fiverr, Freelancer or Peopleperhour.

Tips for bloggers

1. **Follow a few bloggers who publish regularly and have a steady flow of income from publications such as Medium or Huffington Post or Business Partner Magazine.** It's easier if you find someone whose work you admire and whose topic interests you. But it doesn't have to be in your field of interest. As long as the blog format is good you can learn from it. The important thing is to note what and how regularly they publish and their style or voice in their market. Pay particular attention to attention-grabbing headlines – you must be able to get people to read that first sentence! By focusing on just a few experts, you will gain expertise without being distracted by the hundreds of people who want to bag you as a client. Learn as much as possible using freebie resources.

2. Set an objective to **write an article per day / week**. Set aside a day to do this.

3. **FOCUS.** The favourite word of Bill Gates and Warren Buffet. Put your phone on airplane mode or use the Tree app to set time aside whilst you work (you plant a tree to grow in one hour or four hours). If you leave the app in that time your tree dies so it serves as an incentive to stay offline in the app for the time you require to write your article. Productivity and perseverance are key to success. You live in an era where you're bombarded constantly by people getting in your space trying to sell you things or grab your attention. If you're constantly distracted you won't get into the flow or achieve your objective.

4. **DISCIPLINE.** Be consistent. If you work four hours uninterrupted daily aiming to finish a piece of content each time, you will soon have a portfolio of work to show for your efforts. People will pay you money in exchange for your reputation and the value you offer.

5. **Be honest with yourself about your strengths and weaknesses.** If you can put your ideas in print without too many ups and downs, or without becoming so disheartened it interferes with your productivity for the rest of that week, then that's great. If you're easily distracted and not a completer-finisher, take steps to ensure you tick things off the list. You don't want certain aspects of your personality to interfere with your long-term goals or get in the way of daily actions towards your short-term goals.

6. **BE YOURSELF.** The more real your voice, the more you believe in what you write, the more your followers will grow. Also, by sharing from a desire to help you will find followers organically. If you share the content of other bloggers because you like it and feel that it genuinely helps, you will quickly find followers amongst fellow bloggers too who will support you back.

Next steps if this is for you

There are some important points to bear in mind if you decide to go down the route of writing to make money.

This route would definitely start out as a side-gig rather than a full-time job (read about the Gig Economy in Chapter 11).

- **Don't expect to earn money from writing for the first year or two.** Building a following takes time and a lot of hard work. It doesn't provide an instantaneous income. If you begin now and find a highly engaged tribe of people who love what you're writing, in a year or two you can expect to monetise the account. Don't be disheartened by this. You have to start somewhere. Even the most famous influencer bloggers wrote their first blog on day one and published it to an audience of family members! Many successful bloggers were busy multi-tasking when they started out, studying or working jobs and writing in their spare time. If you love writing, start today. Fear of change will turn on your mental emergency break, you have to get past that. The only move is the next one!

- If you're unsure where to start, do a keyword research based on what people want to know in relation to your topic. Then make sure you use high-value keywords in your blog title and within your content. This will help you up your game as your start out and maximise your SEO, helping people to find your blog. Check out www.adamenfroy.com for tips on making money online covering everything from blogging to becoming a business owner.

- Write. This sounds obvious but you will only be successful in this environment if you are productive. DO THE WORK. Don't grumble about not getting anywhere if you haven't slogged through hours preparing content. Tim Denning www.timdenning.com, of Medium and Huffington Post, has online training where he talks you through how to formulate the article to get it published in a magazine or other publication. It helps to have a strategy. You can't sit around hoping to be published in a respected magazine. Study the format, **how to crush the headline, how to write an interesting sub-heading, how to formulate the main points of the article and then build the article around that. You're not in the hope market. Don't sit around hoping to become a writer/blogger – prepare and produce, then ask!**

People will find and read your content more easily if it is advertised on platforms like Facebook, Instagram, Medium (the online magazine) and Twitter. Remember the 2Cs: content and consistency. Write quality content and be sure to write consistently so that you have a body of work to show which helps your negotiating power. Don't approach major publications until you have some experience of writing for smaller publishers. Once your articles are discovered in a magazine or on a popular blog (someone else's) and people start to follow you, you can direct them to your own blog and continue from there.

CHAPTER 2
ECOMMERCE

HOW JACK BLOOMFIELD HARBOURED A PASSION FOR BUSINESS FROM THE AGE OF EIGHT, BECOMING AN AUSSIE MILLIONAIRE BEFORE FINISHING HIGH SCHOOL

Jack was laser-focused on earning his own money from a young age, mowing the neighbours' lawns and selling goodie bags from a stand at his parents' tennis club amongst many money-making schemes. He admits that he didn't distinguish himself particularly at school, but he was passionate about his business ventures and always dreaming up new ways of earning (https://7news.com.au/spotlight/teen-millionaires-the-kids-running-successful-businesses-who-say-you-can-too-c-414921). By the time he was twelve, Jack had already created his first app and at fifteen, he began his career in eCommerce selling products online ranging from flashlights to money clips. Today he is heavily involved in operating and growing eCommerce businesses. He is the Founder and CEO of Disputify, a fintech startup which scans eCommerce activity to pre-empt and stop fraudulent transactions, protecting online businesses and saving them time and money. Check Jack out here: https://www.jackbloomfield.com.au.

About eCommerce

The birth of eCommerce dates back to the 3rd of April 1995 when John Wainwright, an Australian software engineer, decided to buy a book called *Fluid Concepts / Creative Analogies: Computer Models of the Fundamental Mechanisms of Thought*, in the process becoming Amazon's first ever customer. The Wainwright Building at 535 Terry Avenue North in Seattle is named after him. Not bad for indulging in a little bit of retail therapy! Today, twenty five years later, as news outlets report more closures of offline retail businesses, the eCommerce industry makes US$4.2 billion (£3.1 billion) worldwide and the future of e-business continues to shine bright. The next ten years will bring even more exciting opportunities as cutting-edge brands experiment with digital commerce. Voice commerce and headless commerce as well as live stream and video game-enabled businesses will bring more opportunities to earn and contribute to the economy.

Electronic commerce is a business model that allows you to buy and sell things on the internet. You can either sell products via a website, as long as it can securely take payments, or you can build a dedicated shop on eCommerce platforms such as Shopify, ShopWired, BigCommerce, WooCommerce. There are four traditional eCommerce business models:

1. B2C (business to consumer). This refers to anything you buy online as a consumer from a t-shirt to art.
2. B2B (business to business). This is where a business sells its products and services to another business (which sells the goods on or is the end-user themselves).
3. C2B (consumer to business). In the C2B model, consumers post work that they need to have done and businesses directly compete to do the work. This is the principle behind Upwork, a company that helps businesses source freelancers.
4. C2C (consumer to consumer). In this eCommerce model, a business connects consumers and charges a fee for the pleasure. Companies like eBay and Depop are big in this area.

The eCommerce model that features predominantly in this chapter is B2C, but it's the delivery method that has disrupted the market and lowered barriers into the business, making it easy for young adults to enter the market with little capital investment. **The newest delivery method is dropshipping, where you market and sell items fulfilled by a third-party supplier, like eBay or AliExpress.** It's a good way for young people to start their own business because

a) You don't need capital to purchase items you sell; and
b) You don't hold inventory, so you don't need a warehouse to store goods.

In short, **you don't stock or own the inventory which you sell in your Online Shop.** You advertise a product and only purchase that item from a third party when a buyer clicks the 'buy' button in your shop. Once this happens, a purchase notification is sent to your online store and you then send the purchase order to the third-party supplier with instructions to ship the product directly to the customer. As the seller, you don't have to handle the product directly. Dropshipping differs from the standard retail model in that the seller doesn't stock or own inventory, purchasing on demand from a third-party such as a manufacturer or wholesaler to fulfil a customer order. **With dropshipping, it's relatively painless to get into eCommerce because you're not holding the merchandise.**

If you like to stay on top of retail trends, you're good at spotting gaps in the market and you think quickly and act quickly, then a career in eCommerce might suit you. Two young entrepreneurial Australians did all these things at the beginning of April 2020, spotting a gap in the market caused by huge numbers of people being confined to their homes during lockdown.

> HOW LACHLAN DELCHAU-JONES AND TAYLOR REILLY, TWO ENTREPRENEURIAL TEENS FROM BRISBANE, SPOTTED AN OPPORTUNITY IN THE MARKET DURING LOCKDOWN THAT NETTED THEM AUS$70K IN A MONTH

On April 10th, 2020, eighteen-year-old Lachlan Delchau-Jones, called his business partner Taylor Reilly, nineteen, announcing that he'd just watched a news segment on staying occupied during lockdown. The news item sparked an idea that led to them building a business overnight. Using a retail method called dropshipping, the pair sourced products in the arts and crafts niche from a third-party supplier in China which the supplier shipped to their clients for them. Taylor and Lachlan credit their success in this particular venture (just one arm of a larger entrepreneurial effort) to the fact that lockdown saw extraordinary numbers of Australians spending extended time at home and getting their retail therapy fix online rather than offline. Both young men had been interested in business and making money from an early age. Lachlan had paid for an expensive eCommerce course from his pocket money when he was fourteen years old and had already earned a reputation at school for making money online. When they met at a party in their late teens, something clicked and they decided to go into partnership.

Eight steps to opening an online shop

1. <u>Learn Everything about eCommerce</u>
    To avoid the newbie mistakes we all make when entering an unfamiliar market, there are excellent online courses that teach you everything you need to know about eCommerce. Udemy and ECommerce Training Academy offer courses. Next, network for all you're worth! There are lots of online communities dealing purely with eCommerce. Facebook Groups are great for networking. Check out the *Build a Store in 21 Days* or *Double My ECommerce Sales in 12 Months* Groups. There are plenty of great blogs by people doing eCommerce. Follow a few of these. It's the quickest way to learn. In particular, take a look at the Shopify blog and the ECommerce Training Academy blog. Read e-guides like 30 Ways to Make Your First Sale at <u>www.shopify.ca/blog/make-your-first-sale</u> or The Ultimate Guide to Dropshipping at

www.shopify.ca/blog/dropshipping-guide. Check out articles and read books such as *Kick-Ass Social Commerce for E-preneurs: It's Not About Likes — It's About Sales* by John Lawson and Debra Schepp. Attend webinars and eCommerce events.

2. <u>Decide on your Niche</u>
Your niche is your target audience, your particular customer base. Put some thought into deciding who your niche audience is. If you're starting from scratch, you will be choosing products based on your niche audience. How old are they, male or female or both, what do they like to do in their spare time, what do they buy normally? Keep your target audience in mind and research what they're buying online. You'll need a detailed description of your customer and what they buy. **Choosing your niche is like buying a gift for someone you know very well. You think about what they love to do, where they hang out, what they talk about and then buy a gift for them based on their likes. If you want your target audience to buy from you, only buy with that person in mind and stock your store with things they love.** Check out https://neilpatel.com/blog/choosingECommerce-niche/.

3. <u>Brainstorm what to call your business</u>
The name of your business is important. Ensure that the name and email address are the same or similar, and when you choose a domain name, make sure

it matches or closely approximates the name of your shop. Remember when choosing a name:

- keep it pertinent to what your selling
- choose a name people can remember how to spell so they can find you easily; and
- choose a business name that you can buy a domain name for (see above).

4. <u>Choose between dropshipping or direct to consumer</u>
    The Direct to Consumer delivery method involves you holding the products, which will require warehousing and certainly a certain amount of capital investment upfront. Some shop owners might choose direct to consumer over dropshipping, because not being in control of the supply chain can cause issues if there's a problem with the product or delivery of the product. Having a good relationship with a supplier (or, at the least, direct access to them) is not always possible using dropshipping, with the result that you can't guarantee customer satisfaction every time.

5. <u>Choosing an eCommerce Platform</u>
    Nothing beats the experience of opening your own shop in the online space. The five top platforms to host small businesses are Shopify, BigCommerce, WooCommerce, Wix and Squarespace. **Whichever platform you choose, they do all the hard work for you.** I'm familiar with Shopify, which is easy to set up, offers an array of apps and the Shopify Team are very supportive. ECommerce startup costs can be deliberately kept to a minimum, but you will need to pay Shopify (or equivalent) a monthly fee for hosting your shop (with monthly charges ranging from US$29 or £22

for a basic account up to US$299 or £227 for an advanced plan). The basic plan gives you everything you require when starting out. You will need to have a running inventory balance (not necessary if you use dropshipping), a domain name that will cost about US$15 or £12 per year and some kind of payment processing which can be done through Shopify (or via PayPal if you have an account already).

6. <u>Choosing products to sell</u>
So now that you've chosen your niche and you have a name and URL for your business, you'll need products to sell. **Find social proof in your niche. Check out the eBay and AliExpress´ best-seller lists.** Check out bestsellers in your niche on Google and the most well-received items in your niche on Amazon's best-seller list. Avoid name brands (if people want a headset, they will have a particular brand in mind), think of selling at a 20% to 50% margin if possible. Choose a product you know something about (it will make it more fun for you to research items you're interested in personally). For product ideas, search for *trending products* and read as many articles as you can. Check out this Bold Commerce article for profitable products to sell online in 2020 here https://blog.boldcommerce.com/what-to-sell-online-trending-products.
Keep your eyes and ears open and try to spot gaps in the market and anticipate trends for certain products at certain times. Remember, give the customer what they want. This will help to

quickly monetise your efforts. Having decided that arts and crafts goods would be in demand over lockdown, Taylor and Lachlan quickly hooked up with a supplier in China. Next, they had the goods sent to them so they could be checked for quality. Choosing a product that is well made with a high perceived value is important as you will be marking up the product to sell to your customers from a platform like Shopify and you want to provide value to your customers. Take your own photos of the product for your ad campaign. **Don't build a store based solely on what you want to buy and what you're interested in. Pay close attention to what's happening in the world around you and adapt what you're selling to meet demand.**

7. <u>Choosing a supplier</u>
    According to Lachlan, establishing a relationship with your supplier can be the difference between the success and failure of your business venture and is a key part of doing eCommerce using dropshipping as a delivery method. He and Taylor managed to get a direct line number for their supplier so they could Whats App directly if there was a problem. The value of a direct line of contact to the supply chain is not obvious until there are problems, either with the product itself or delivery of the product, and your customer looks to you to rectify the issue. **The biggest setbacks in dropshipping will come about either because of non-delivery of**

the product or because a faulty spec is delivered to your client.

8. <u>Marketing your shop</u>
    The main rule here is to have a presence where your consumers are hanging out. For example, if they're on Instagram choose that channel only and start small. Link your social media to your store by adding your Facebook pixel to Shopify or Woo Commerce or whatever platform you're using.

    You can pay for ads too. You can even expect a 100% return on investment for ads according to Google's Economic Impact Report. Read articles on pay per click analysis. Use Facebook Ads and AdWords. In Taylor and Lachlan's case, they sourced their supplier of arts and crafts in China, built a website about the business and product, then set up Facebook marketing to run ads for the product online and direct traffic back to their website and the buy button. Many young entrepreneurs are sourcing products on AliExpress (China's version of eBay) but some have either stopped sourcing products from China (because of perceived problems with delivery times and supply) or have chosen not to get involved with that market (choosing eBay or similar instead). Give yourself twelve to eighteen months to make a profit. Finding the right product can take time.

<u>Costs</u>
Naturally, there are monthly costs involved in having a shop on a dedicated eCommerce platform, whether or not your product is selling yet. **Driving traffic to your product from ads on Facebook is a key**

part of the dropshipping operation and these costs will also have to be factored in unless you have a huge list and can count on organic traffic! Your domain name is paid for yearly and all of these costs add up. Until you have customers hitting the buy button in your shop, such costs may be draining your resources. As with any business venture, you should consult an accountant to understand your tax position and to register for VAT (not applicable in the US). In the UK for example, you must be VAT registered for sales of over £85k.

Another advantage to having a thriving eCommerce business is that it affords you opportunities for other income streams. Once a shop is running itself effectively on twenty to thirty hours input per week, or once fulfilment of the orders has been outsourced, some highly successful eCommerce entrepreneurs have turned their hand to teaching (another perfect example of a pivot) where they teach students how to run an online store.

Next steps if this is for you

Dedicated eCommerce platforms can be used as online learning tools, with huge libraries of videos to help you navigate eCommerce. Learn as much as you can about your chosen area (preferably by doing a course) then sign up for a free trial on an eCommerce platform. Many platforms have free trial periods (Shopify has a 90-day free trial for example). If you decide to set up your store on WordPress, you'll need to host your site using hosting providers such as A2 Hosting, SiteGround and InMotion and use plugins like WooCommerce so you can take payments securely. Check out www.websitebuilderexpert.com. If you don't use a dedicated eCommerce platform, bear in mind that your website will be the face of your brand so find a good website designer.

If you're not quite ready to take on a startup but can see this in your future, you might want to **approach one of the larger eCommerce businesses for a role within their company.** Many successful business owners in eCommerce kickstarted their careers by learning the business from the inside, working for large eCommerce companies before pivoting to set up their own business. Also, consider working for startups. If you find an interesting startup, it can be a very lucrative way to kickstart your career as you get first-hand experience of so many different parts of the business.

Global retail sales in eCommerce are projected to grow to US$6.5 trillion by 2022. The industry has now taken on a life of its own, with sales reaching epic proportions during the pandemic. **Perhaps you have your own jewellery or knitted hats to sell or think that your Aunt's miniature paintings would sell well in an online store, or have an idea for a gadget that you found in Thailand, which you think your audience might love if it were marketed here.** If you have an idea of a product to sell and you can invest money in setting up a shop on an eCommerce platform, this is a hugely educational way to kickstart your career and learn a tonne of things about running a business.

CHAPTER 3
PODCASTING

HOW A SEVENTEEN-YEAR-OLD NEW YORKER, BECAME THE YOUNGEST PERSON EVER TO HAVE A SYNDICATED PODCAST FOR iHEART.

When Sammy Jaye was thirteen years old, she got to pitch an idea for her dream podcast to someone at iHeart radio station in New York. They loved it. She used to listen to podcasts whilst cleaning her bedroom and had spotted a gap in the teen market never thinking that it would get picked up by the station. She did a test interview with Jordan Fisher and so began her record-breaking journey into podcasting https://www.refinery29.com/en-us/2020/02/9350277/lets-be-real-with-sammy-jaye-podcast). In her podcast, "Let's be real with Sammy Jaye", Sammy interviews famous guests about everything from political activism to mental health. She is smart and disarming and with her can-do attitude, she delivers honest, unfiltered interviews with athletes, musicians, activists and entrepreneurs. At fourteen years old (whilst still in 8th Grade) Sammy began working with Radio Disney as their East Coast correspondent, doing all their social and digital video content. She recorded the pilot of her podcast at sixteen which went to series when she was seventeen. She illustrates perfectly the tireless quest to get stuff done and tick things off her list required to be a successful entrepreneur, influencer or freelancer. Sammy is passionate about her work, focused on her career and level-headed about using her mentors to constantly bounce around ideas and push boundaries. Check her out here: https://www.iheart.com/podcast/1248-lets-be-real-with-sammy-j-56806419/.

Another podcaster making waves in this space is twenty-two-year-old Andrew 'Apple' Crider. Apple adds value to the lives of young entrepreneurs keen to make a success of their careers with his podcast "Young Smart Money". Read about Apple below.

HOW ANDREW 'APPLE' CRIDER BUILT HIS REPUTATION AS THE HOST OF THE PODCAST "YOUNG SMART MONEY", TO INFORM AMBITIOUS YOUNG PEOPLE WHAT IT TAKES TO BECOME A SUCCESSFUL ENTREPRENEUR AND CREATE FINANCIAL FREEDOM

Apple Crider was always entrepreneurial and whilst in his teens this spirit saw him investigating Amazon FBA (Fulfilment by Amazon) Solutions. He soon realised that he would rather use his skills to solve problems for people, establishing his social media agency soon after and eventually founding "Young Smart Money", which is tailored to young people interested in the world of entrepreneurship and non-traditional ways of earning a living. He serves his followers with informative interviews in which he contrasts the work of successful startup founders with the work of social media influencers, helping young people to understand key parts of these businesses and how to grow them. With a blend of financial and career advice and in-depth interviews that cut straight to the essentials, Young Smart Money is a podcast born of its time, filling a much-needed space to help young people solve problems, get smart about money and crucially to bridge the gap between education and earning a successful living. Well worth tuning into! Check Apple out here: https://www.stitcher.com/show/young-smart-money. Also, on www.applecrider.com.

Apple makes it clear that setting up an online business and making a name for yourself is a major project. A huge amount of groundwork is carried out and long hours invested before you get noticed in a space. **The steps to succeed in the online space require focus and discipline, a fact that is often glossed over and which results in many young people mistakenly viewing online work (particularly the work of influencers but also of entrepreneurs) as a way to make easy money** because they see young people making money seemingly effortlessly. The people you see raking in the money and living a seemingly carefree life have been proactively and consistently chasing their dreams for some time, for some since they were thirteen or fourteen years old.

Podcasting is a good way to earn a living if you like people, enjoy chatting to them and finding out things about their life and have a particular interest or hobby to base your podcast around, like gaming or sport or managing money. Apple's podcasts are fun and engaging but he asks his guests penetrating questions about his subject offering real insight to his audience who lap it up.

Seven steps to starting a podcast

Podcasting requires a small financial investment upfront, but this will pay dividends later, as long as you're passionate about your subject and do it consistently over time. Many of the courses on podcasting are paid-for but check out GarageBand Free Podcasting Training on LinkedIn Learning here:
https://www.linkedin.com/learning/topics/garageband.
Udemy has a number of podcasting courses one of which is called Podcasting Made Easy – How to Start a Podcast. Check it out here:
https://www.udemy.com/course/how-to-start-a-podcast-x/

1.   Deciding the Mission, Name and Aims
Working out your "why" is important and it's advisable to keep this in front of you when you're deciding on the name and the episodes. It will guide the content of the shows and also keep you motivated when you're struggling with a theme or getting a show out. Deciding who the podcast is for is equally important. Are you an experienced gamer? Then your target audience might be thirteen- to twenty-two-year-olds interested in gaming. If you're a personal trainer, then your audience might be interested in training to run a marathon or perhaps bodybuilding. If you're a hobbyist, then your target audience will be anyone who shares your passion such as guitar playing or mountain biking. If you already

have an audience from something else you do, then you can survey them to find out what they want to hear more about or what they're struggling with and plan your podcast around that.

Most people start with no audience and the first few episodes will be just talking to your family! Nothing drastic happens! You have to start somewhere and when they do find you, new listeners don't care if they've not heard of you before as long as your content is good. You'll find your tribe by providing valuable insights, whether it's gaming tips or an interview with an expert in your target field.

Your podcast's description is really important to attract listeners to your show. Take time to write the perfect summary. Finally, the name is equally important. Don't be too clever as people need to be able to find the podcast when they're searching for information about your specialty area. Equally, it's not advisable to use your own name as no-one will know what you're broadcasting about, although you could potentially call it "White Water Rafting with "Jane Public".

2. <u>Planning the content and episode structure</u>
Decide on the length of the podcast. Anything from twenty minutes to one hour. It's helpful if the podcast is consumable for the length of a commute or a car journey, say twenty to thirty minutes, but the episode length should be decided by the content and the audience, so work out the length based on these two elements. Episodes should be as frequent as possible if you're trying to attract followers, but fortnightly or monthly is the minimum. So not less than twelve podcasts in the year.

It's like anything, if you're going to do it, do it seriously and approach it as you would a job. **Make sure it's clear what each episode is about,** such as "Five simple things to do when approaching rapids to protect your crew". Finally, the podcast format will be either just you or you and a co-host or you and the interviewee. Other formats include round table discussions and even documentary-style podcasts.

3.   <u>Recording the podcast</u>
The first thing is to acquire the equipment. As you're starting out, there's no need to go overboard. **With a Blue Yeti or Samson Q2U microphone, normal ear buds, a webcam and a free subscription to Zoom you're all set to go** for virtual interviews. A free Zoom account allows you to talk to up to three people for forty minutes and records as you go (remember to hit the record button!). For a larger group of people and a longer discussion, you will need to upgrade to a paid Zoom membership. For in-person interviews, Audacity is free software that you can use on your computer to record and edit the audio once you plug your mic in. By the way, Mac users have a bit of an advantage here as you may have GarageBand installed by default on your Mac. With your mic at the ready and your editing software installed you can hit record! According to Colin Gray of The Podcast Host, if you're doing lots of interviews, the Rode Smartlav+ lapel microphone turns your smartphone into a mobile mic recorder giving close-up and consistent recordings of speech. Later you could update your set to a digital recorder like a Zoom H6 or a mixer such as the Yamaha

MG10 but there is no need to spend lots of money at this stage.

4.   <u>Scripting the podcast</u>
Reading from a script may sound dull given that podcasting is, by its nature, more suited to a conversational style but **a script can make the difference between sounding professional or not.** Be careful if you script the show to ensure you sound natural and engaging.

5.   <u>Editing the podcast</u>
If you're using Audacity this also works for producing the show. If you have savings from a part-time job or financial backing, you could consider paying someone else to edit the podcast for you. Fiverr (for one-time jobs) and Upwork (for longer-term freelancer work) have lots of skilled people willing to provide services to entrepreneurs. You can source music for your podcast (legally) from a range of sites. **Look up licensed music under "creative commons" or find free podcast music on Incompetech (music by Kevin MacLeod).** It's an amazing free resource (the only quid pro quo is that you attribute the work) but a lot of Kevin's songs are so popular and have been used so much that they're easily recognisable. A young friend of mine uses BenSound to edit her work. **BenSound is a library of music that is also free to use as long as you give credit to his music. In the YouTube Create Studio, there is also a library of songs and sound effects that you can download and use for free.** There are other sites to source podcast music, but most are paid-for options. Like many sign-up/subscription services, you can

sign up, download music you like then cancel after a month. Search "how to find podcast music" online.

6.   <u>Publishing the podcast</u>
You'll need cover art that you can produce (for free!) on Canva. Or if you don't fancy designing a cover you could outsource the design to a freelancer on Fiverr. Your cover should be 1400 x 1400 pixels, in PNG or JPG form and under 500 kb in size (check out Colin Gray at the podcasthost.com). You'll need to host your podcast on a hosting platform such as Captivate, Buzzsprout or Transistor. These range from 12–20 GBP/USD per month. You'll either place one of these hosting providers on your website or have a website set up on their site. Then all that's left is to submit your podcast to various directories so people can find you. Whichever platform is hosting you will have direct routes to get your podcast playing on Spotify, Apple Podcasts, etc. Most podcasting courses will teach you about building your audience and also how to monetise your podcast.

7.   <u>Monetising the podcast</u>
Sponsorship is the most common way that podcasters make money. Brands will pay you to promote their products or services during your show. It won't surprise you to learn that the more listeners you have the better. How much you earn from a sponsor depends on the number of downloads your episodes get. Using social media platforms to drive traffic to your podcast is commonplace.

Apple Crider's Tips for podcasting and monetising your show

- Naming the podcast. You have to know what the show is about just by reading the name. Ask yourself what's the value proposition and who are you trying to reach? Is it clear in the name? Go to the top fifty podcasts and check out names for inspiration. Set a timer and do it in thirty minutes.

- Pay a professional to do channel art. Find examples you like and show them to someone on Fiverr, and that's it, done.

- Monetising the show. **Plenty of podcasters know how to get listeners but not how to turn that attention into income.** At the front end you could be doing affiliate marketing, promoting products you use and endorse vis a vis the microphone, the software you use. You could be selling something to your audience e.g. a book or a course or you could have sponsors on your show★. At the back end you could provide marketing services to your guests. If your guests are businesspeople selling products in the online space, what would be helpful to them? You could help them with digital marketing or offer them PR agency skills or social media marketing. Download a free cheat sheet called *15 Ways to Monetise Your Podcast* here: www.applecrider.com.

- Publishing. Anchor.fm is a free site that will distribute your podcast to Google podcast, Apple podcast, Spotify, Stitcher and more.

- Marketing. Leverage other people's platforms to grow your show. Your interviewees will help build your show. Make your guests look good in the interview. Let them talk about their passion. Make it easy for others to promote your show. After the interview create simple graphics with a photo of the guest to promote the podcast.

* Apple has never put a sponsor on his show and doesn't monetise at the front end because he's not convinced it provides value for his listeners. Do what feels right for you.

Next steps if this is for you

Podcasting is not only big business but it's attainable if you're good with people and hit on a good idea for a show. Anyone with a microphone, a webcam and ear buds can have a show with generally high quality but don't get hung up on it being perfect. The more shows you produce the better they get.

There is Podcast Launch Training available on Teachable but there's also plenty of free material so check that out first. Check out *How to Plan your Podcast* with Colin Gray on the following link:
https://www.podcast.co/inspire/colin-gray-the-podcast-host.
Check out Podcast Nation, Podcast Movement and Apple Crider on Facebook.

In the meantime, tuning into smart podcasts is an easy way both to have fun and research ideas and themes for your own show. Tune in whilst you're on a long drive, doing chores or at the gym. Choose from an array of podcasts, from breakthroughs in science to YouTube culture. Here are some interesting ones:

- **The 80,000 Hours Podcast** – Hosted by Rob Wiblin, this podcast is all about using your career to solve real-world problems. Expect debates from rogue AI to climate change.

- **The Moth** – This is for you if you like storytelling or are interested in pursuing writing for a career. It promotes the art of storytelling by inviting guests to appear live and tell their stories without notes. The podcast collects performances making them available to a wider audience.

- **Radiolab** – Hosts Robert and Jad break down scientific concepts (and philosophical ones) to make them more accessible.

- **Mental Music** – This podcast focuses on mental health covering topics from social media to lack of sleep to how sound affects your daily life.

- **Dear Hank and John** – Brothers Hank and John Green answer questions you might like help with, such as how to quit a job or how to find time to do little things as well as more whacky stuff. John Green is the author of The Fault in our Stars.

- **Song Exploder** – If you're a future songwriter or a music fan this is for you. It features guest interviews with musicians like FKA Twigs, who pick apart their own songs and explain how they composed them.

- **Socially Awkward** – Zac and Justin are on a mission to show that we all feel like freaks sometimes! You don't need to be socially awkward to have a good laugh!

50

CHAPTER 4
YOUTUBE

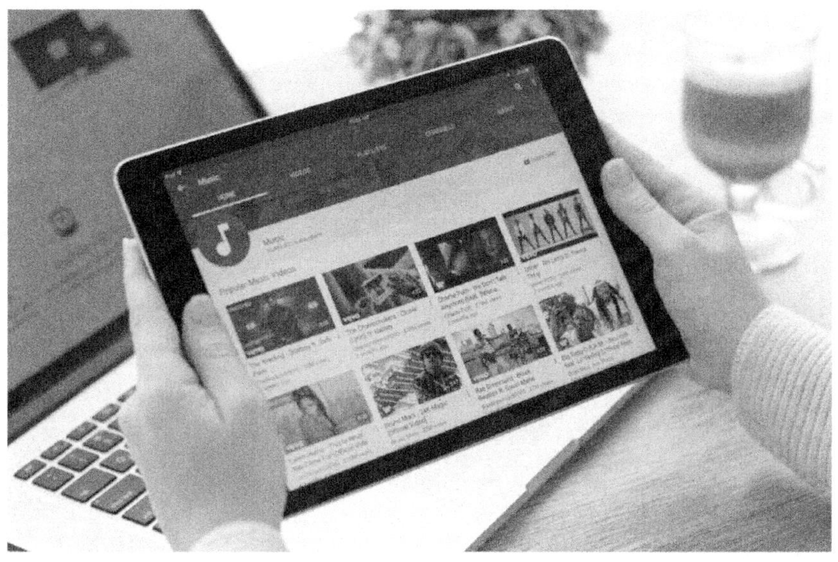

HOW AN ENTERPRISING YOUNG BRITISH WOMAN BECAME ONE OF THE MOST SUCCESSFUL BEAUTY AND FASHION VLOGGERS IN THE UK.

In 2008 a twenty-year-old British girl watched an interview with Taylor Swift in which Taylor said that she watched makeup tutorials in her spare time. She discovered YouTube as a result of watching that interview and decided to have a go at making videos (https://www.theguardian.com/careers/2015/nov/18/fleur-de-force-career-fashion-beauty-vlogger). The young girl was Fleur de Force and today Fleur is a full-time beauty and fashion vlogger with three YouTube Channels and more than 1.39m subscribers. Like many successful influencers, her business has expanded to include writing books and launching collaborations with MAC cosmetics and Eylure amongst others. She has won a host of awards including Best Beauty YouTuber and the Johnson and Johnson Beauty Journalism Award and is a regular keynote speaker at various international events. Any influencer will tell you that becoming successful requires full-time commitment, often exceeding the eight-hour days of working in an office. Fleur openly admits that her work, particularly in the early days, took up more time than a nine-to-five job but that, for her, it never feels like work. She is passionate about her subject and providing value for her followers which drives her work commitment. Check Fleur out here: https://www.fleurdeforce.com.

YouTube can provide huge rewards for channels that get a lot of views. The most successful YouTubers make a significant amount of money while seemingly having lots of fun (like gaming or setting challenges). Yet YouTube is a long game and not without its challenges. In a busy space, getting views requires dedication. Increasing YouTube views and subscribers involves content being spot-on and channel art being cool and matching the channel theme. There are coaches and online courses that teach you how to do this but before investing in a course, consider whether you have the material to post constantly on your own YouTube channel. Give careful thought to:

- Your market e.g. online gaming,
- Your ideal customer or avatar (for this example: ` teenage boys age thirteen to eighteen years),
- Your subject (e.g. Minecraft tutorials).

People make YouTube videos about all sorts of weird and wonderful things from making tiny food in a tiny kitchen to computer gadget reviews and from making parodies of other peoples' videos to touching objects with a live mic! The highest-paid YouTube star according to Forbes magazine is nine-year-old Ryan Kaji whose topic is toy reviews. Ryan earned US$26 million in 2019 from his toy review and lifestyle channels, growing his subscriber base to 25.8 million.

https://www.businessinsider.com/ryans-world-boy-makes-26-million-per-year-on-youtube-2019-12?r=US&IR=T

Today Ryan's YouTube channel "Ryan's World" has grown beyond a channel into a huge business in clothing, magazines, fast-food toys, television (he has a show on Nick Jr) and more. With eighty brands licensed to the family's empire, Ryan's face appears on tv, on toothbrushes, on video games and magazines and all over the internet. **According to Forbes magazine, a major portion of Ryan's income comes from ads in his videos** (a reported 96% of his income is from ads, with 4% coming from sponsored posts). Ryan's brand is a multi-million-dollar franchise.

If you're considering building a YouTube Channel, the eight most popular YouTube video topics include:

- Entertainment
- Food
- Gaming
- Beauty and Fashion
- Music
- Sports
- Science and Technology
- Travel

Once you've chosen a topic and some hip channel art, it's time to focus on having good quality video content and lots of ideas around your theme. Then it's simply a matter of getting in front of the camera! If you can produce lots of five-to-ten-minute videos (that get hits) every week, after a year you can generate money from your channel via ads. Find a list of video ideas generating a lot of income for YouTubers below with tips to help you get started.

YouTube video ideas for your business

For some of the best YouTube content around visit the aptly named www.designwizard.com.

Unboxing

This video format continues to rank amongst the very popular YouTube ideas. It's a favourite with kids (like RyanToys Review, now known as Ryan's World) so is suitable for a younger viewer. However, there is also a version for the more mature audience e.g. the Unbox Therapy channel.

Educational

Like it says on the box! these videos teach something e.g. you could teach teenagers how to choose subjects for A-Levels. Be sure to use infographics and vivid images to explain the points you make.

Rant

You've all seen one! It's not something you need to consider in advance. If you're angry about something, you'll easily be able to rant about it on video. Recently a video posted during lockdown went viral. It was of a tearful nurse outside an empty supermarket berating selfish shoppers for stockpiling food leaving her without anything to eat at the end of a stressful twelve-hour shift.

Product review

Featuring a newly released product on your channel can

garner huge views. Tech reviews are hugely popular (see below). Share your own experience of the product and try to stand out from others with engaging commentary. Ben Boxer is a YouTube star who started a successful YouTube channel reviewing technology and unwrapping computer gadgets for his audience.

Vlogs

A vlog will allow you to talk about your life and what interests you. It can be difficult to get off the ground but if you manage it, it's rewarding. Your content will need to be current and interesting but more importantly you need to be genuine and connect to your audience. Fleur has more than 170m page views across her three YouTube channels. Her advice: "If you want to be a YouTuber be yourself. It's not like being a TV presenter. They [the audience] feel like you have a personal connection with them. It's real and raw." From: Dream Jobs, Interview by Charlotte Seager www.theguardian.co.uk 2015.

Pranks

The most successful YouTube category is prank videos and has been for some years. It doesn't need to be a large prank like the most high-profile YouTubers get up to! Smaller pranks can be just as entertaining. Many YouTubers prank their family and friends starting out. There's a really funny video that went viral recently of a father yelling at his brood because he thinks they've kicked a ball and cracked the new 85" TV screen.

There are lots of other ideas for YouTube channels, such as discussion, tips, cute videos of your cat, life hacks, celebrity gossip videos or product launches. Check out Michael Cole's "100 Best YouTube Videos for 2020" here: https://www.designwizard.com/blog/100-best-youtube.

Monetising your YouTube channel

There are hundreds of YouTubers with thousands of watch hours and thousands of followers who are not monetising their YouTube channel. The fact is that some people on YouTube earn nothing or barely anything whilst others, such as Ryan, Pewdiepie and Markiplier, are earning millions of dollars per year. If you do have a considerable following on your channel, brands will pay you in the region of $20-$50 dollars for every few thousand views they get on your channel. Check out the list below for information on how to monetise your YouTube channel.

Earning from ads

This is a big source of revenue for YouTubers. Once you become a YouTube partner, you earn money from ad placement. **You can earn from ads which run before your videos or from Google AdSense banner ads.** To become a partner you must have a minimum of 4k video watch hours on your channel and a minimum of 1k subscribers. You can accumulate the 4k hours over any timeframe. The hit "Gangnam Style" took 5 months to achieve 1 billion views.

Affiliate Links

Much like promoting on your blog, you can post an affiliate link in your video description and speak about the link in your videos. This works particularly well with educational videos and informative product reviews. There are lot of affiliate programmes to choose from or choose an affiliate network which will join you to many different programmes in one place e.g. shareasale. Choose affiliate links carefully not just for the monetary benefit. Your viewers will only follow links from a trusted source. You will earn commission once a viewer visits your link to buy.

<u>Use SEO (Search Engine Optimisation)</u>
If you're just starting out, you will need to be quite strategic and maximise your SEO to kickstart your earnings on YouTube. As you would when looking for ideas for a blog, do a keyword research and find out what people are searching for on YouTube. Then make sure to use high-value keywords in the tags, title and description. If you've uploaded lots of videos, you can check your "traffic source" to find out what people are searching for when they find your videos.

<u>Become an Amazon Influencer</u>
If you have thousands of followers already, you can join the Amazon Influencer programme where you'll get your own page on Amazon with a link to showcase the products to your followers. When your viewers click through to purchase, you'll receive a commission.

Next steps if this is for you
Many young adults set up YouTube channels with little or no training. If you have something to say or demonstrate, make a video and upload it to YouTube. If you upload a video to YouTube, remember to post on other social media platforms to direct traffic to your video. Every minute 400 tweets go out which include a link to a YouTube video. Do check for copyright infringement. You can use a programme called Automated Content ID which scans over 100 years of video each day.

Don't let fear get in your way. We're all scared of being judged by others but your judgement of yourself is important too. It's hard to live with regret for not having tried something you feel you would be good at. People talk about the risk of doing X or Y, but they rarely talk about the risk of doing nothing. If you have something to share and feel that it's business worthy, it doesn't cost anything to try it. If it's not for you, nothing drastic happens and you've learned something. In an interview with the Guardian Newspaper in 2015, Fleur de Force admitted that when she started out on YouTube, she had no idea how to set about it and it was a huge learning process. "You kind of make it up as you go along which has been difficult but also exciting". Don't underestimate the enormous amount of courage it takes to step into the unknown and try something that you've never done before. But it can be immensely rewarding. Once you attract an audience who want to see more and you begin to earn money from ads on your channel, you can hire people to help you push the boundaries.

An added bonus is that once you've demonstrated your ability in one area other opportunities quickly present themselves. Both Rachel Parcell and Fleur de Force developed multiple income streams ranging from fashion to interior design to authorship, all of which came about from their original, courageous step into the unknown.

CHAPTER 5
INSTAGRAM

HOW ONE YOUNG ENTREPRENEUR'S INGENIOUS USE OF INSTAGRAM AND YOUTUBE TO CONNECT TO HIS AUDIENCE, CHANGED THE COURSE OF MARKETING AND ROCKET-LAUNCHED HIS BUSINESS.

Back in 2012, Ben Francis set up Gymshark, growing it into a multi-million-pound business thanks to social media, namely Instagram and YouTube. Rather than spend money on traditional marketing, Ben set out to impress influential people with his sleek sports kit, recruiting influencers with large followings in the fitness world to promote his product in the online space. Back in 2013, this was pretty cutting edge and gave Ben access to tens of millions of followers and a market ready for cool sportswear. Only nine years ago Ben was a young, gym-obsessed university student with a part-time job delivering pizzas, handstitching gym kit from his family home. Nine years down the line he is worth millions of pounds and has grown Gymshark into one of the most influential sportswear brands in the market. In 2020, Ben hit the Forbes Under 30 list. (https://www.thetimes.co.uk/article/how-ben-francis-built-the-billion-pound-fitness-brand-gymshark-crls00h2n). Check out Gymshark at www.uk.gymshark.com.

As a primarily visual platform, producing visually arresting photos, graphics or art commands attention and followers on Instagram. If you're creative and have a gift for photography or displaying items with flair and panache, then this platform may be right for you. Sara Tasker is a young businesswoman whose creative talents were quickly spotted by her 220k followers.

> HOW ONE YOUNG WOMAN BUILT A PROFITABLE BUSINESS FROM POSTING PHOTOGRAPHS OF HER LIFESTYLE CONTENT TO INSTAGRAM.

Sara Tasker was a speech therapist working for the NHS. In January 2013 whilst on maternity leave, Sara began a challenge to post a photograph per day of her lifestyle content to Instagram (https://www.theguardian.com/money/2017/may/05/earn-a-living-instagram-micro-influencers). Today this Instagrammer, blogger and photographer with 220k followers has become an influencer. She coaches people on how to optimise Instagram for business and is also a podcaster. Sara's story is inspiring because it beautifully illustrates someone doing what they are passionate about and finding a large audience who love it too. It's **also a great example of someone ending up with a lucrative career from an inadvertent moment of sharing on a social**

platform. She has written extensively about "Insta Authenticity". Her book "Hashtag Authentic" is visual and creative and addresses the importance of being real on this platform.

With 500 million-plus daily users, Instagram is a dream not just for social media marketers but, as it's a business network as well as a social network, it's perfect for checking out the job market and finding out what other people your age are doing to make money. Some young adults use Instagram for extra income whilst others make a full-time living from it. With the diversity of the traffic on the platform, there are lots of opportunities to transform your earnings. Before considering ways to monetise Instagram consider the following:

<u>Your business bio</u>
Your bio is one of the first things to be seen when people visit your business account on Instagram. That and your photograph. Ensure you have a winning profile. Let people know exactly what you do and who you are. Make it quirky! Remember to add a link to the website box which is in the business Instagram bio. This is the only place on Instagram where you can add a URL to take a visitor to your website, blog or campaign. Link trees are a way you can add several different URLs if you need more than one. Enable notifications on your account by clicking on the options setting and make sure notifications are on so you can tell when people are interacting with your account.

<u>Your followers</u>
Brands are interested in how many followers you have but also how engaged your followers are with you. But follower count isn't everything. Some brands have done very well with nano-influencers (less than 1k followers),

who have less followers but who are all highly engaged superfans. Advertisers are hungry for influencers to talk glowingly about their products. In the last few years, brands have built tracking features into platforms to make it easier for influencers and companies to track conversions (the number of people who have converted from browser to buyer). It does this by tracking a user's journey from an Instagram account to a brand's website. These metrics allows companies to quantify an influencer's effect on their sales and are used to negotiate influencer agreements. In 2020, even traditional companies like Marks & Spencer in the UK, have turned to influencers to market products.

<u>Who makes money on Instagram?</u>
Brands – More than 25 million businesses use Instagram to promote their products.
Digital Creators – If you have a digital product to sell, you can promote it on Instagram. You can even set up in-app shopping on Instagram and sell your product directly from the platform.
Influencers – we all want personal recommendations for products and services and in the online space influencers are the opinion leaders. If they make a recommendation and you buy a product or service based on that recommendation, they make money.
Instagram Consultants – as with other platforms, if you become a known expert in an area, people will pay you for support and advice. Instagram consultants will advise on creating a winning bio, developing a strategy, monitoring brand awareness, creating capsule captions and much more. There are so many people and businesses on Instagram that it can be difficult to get noticed as you start out – a consultant can help you to grab people's attention.

<u>Best niches for growing your profile on Instagram</u>
Instagram is a powerful sales machine offering all kinds of ways for people to make money on the platform. You can use it to drive traffic to your website and product or use it to document your lifestyle or become an expert in Insta for Business and sell your expertise as an Instagram Consultant. There are hundreds of niche areas (target markets), but the top performing are:

Travelling – Check out @saltinourhair
Beauty – Check out @fleurdeforce
Fashion – Check out @camilacoelho
Lifestyle – Check out @lukasabbat
Health and Fitness – Check out Joe Wicks @thebodycoach
Parenting – Check out @drbeckyathome
Business – Check out @ben.towers
Music – Check out @shekukannehmason
Food – Check out Sammi Manoff @sweetcravings_x
Photography – Check out @amandagrzn

People set up pretty random accounts on Instagram, sometimes just to play with the effect of arbitrarily chosen themes. Sammi Manoff loves experimenting on Instagram. Read her story below:

> HOW SAMMI MANOFF BEGAN POSTING AS A WAY TO EXPRESS HERSELF IN HER EARLY TEENS, GAINING TRACTION FOR HER IMAGES OF SWEETS AND DESSERTS BEFORE BAGGING AN APPRENTICESHIP WITH GOOGLE WHEN SHE DID HER A-LEVELS.

When Sammi Manoff was in her early teens, she was already fascinated by the mechanisms of consumer marketing and, in particular, social media. This led to her setting up an Instagram account based solely on the colour blue just to examine if a random theme, such as the colour blue, could power posts and attract followers (https://www.thejc.com/meet-the-teens-leading-the-way-socially-instagram-influencers-katie-scollan-sammi-manoff-josh-horus-1.479519). It could and did. She got 1000 followers. After completing her A-levels, Sammi subsequently passed a Digital Marketing Apprenticeship at Google with distinction. But long before entering Sixth Form, she launched @sweetcravings_x powered by her passion for food but especially desserts. Posting images of layered chocolate cake and mouth-watering knickerbocker glories, pancakes, sweets and homemade desserts on her account, she garnered more than 2.5k followers and high engagement with her base.

Sammi has a natural ability for seeing the psychological processes and mechanisms at work in social media believing that Instagram works for young people because it provides instant gratification and a visual high. Sammi features here for many reasons not least because she has shown that having a social media presence in 2020 is like a calling card for prestigious companies, a way to prove yourself (in the manner that sitting exams proves another, different set of skills). She is passionate about her subject and she persisted in pursuing her sweets project, posting consistently and building up a dedicated group of followers in the process. Another key take-away from Sammi is that you don't need sky-high numbers of followers to be very successful. Also, anyone who engages in hypotheses testing is deserving of a mention!

Instagram is big business. Never doubt the extent to which it's dictating your life, not just your personal life but also the world around you. It's not only individuals who try to make themselves Insta-ready but the challenge for businesses is to also make their premises, staff and products attractive to social media influencers. Increasingly, companies and Instagram influencers are adapting their approach to make themselves instafriendly by redesigning interiors, hanging plants, propping up inspirational signs, wearing cutting-edge clothing or makeup all in homage to stylised social media. Instagram drives restaurant design, the type of food served (amazing-looking rather than basic good food), even flight patterns as Instagrammers choose to fly to the top destination for Insta photos.

Monetising your Instagram account

- Reach and influence. **A business will pay you as an Instagram user because they want access to your audience.** They hope that your audience will in turn buy from them or recommend the brand to their friends. But reach is only one part of the equation. Influence is also about persuasion i.e. your audience has to take action on what you recommend.

- **A popular way to make money on Instagram is through sponsored posts.** Influencers can set their own rate for working with brands charging from US$5 to hundreds of thousands of dollars per post depending on whether they're a nano influencer (1–9k followers), micro-influencer (10k +), macro-influencer (100k +) or mega-influencer (1m+).

- Sell your own products. This is one of the easiest ways to monetise your Instagram account.

Promote and sell your own courses, e-books, art or jewellery directly from the platform.

- **Become an affiliate.** This is covered elsewhere in this book but selling affiliate products is simply recommending a product using a tracking link. If your followers land on a sales page and make a purchase from an affiliate link on your Instagram site, you get paid. There are so many affiliate programmes to choose from, from Amazon Associates to Commission Junction. Some affiliate programmes are not open to everyone and are dictated by your follower count and other metrics.

- Engagement. If people don't like or share or comment on your posts, you're not striking a chord with them. **An influencer with an engaged audience who likes and endorses a brand, can help the brand grow it's following, increase brand awareness and strongly impact sales.**

Check out "The Step-by-Step Guide to Making Money from Instagram" by Neil Patel. Also, check out Ritvars of www.sellfy.com.

Next steps if this is for you

If you know a lot about Instagram and have effortlessly amassed large audiences, you have lots of options:

- Approach Big Tech, let them see your numbers and clinch a job.
- Set yourself up as an Instagram Consultant and sell your expertise to startups or traditional companies to build their brand in the online space.

- Continue to build your account as an influencer and monetise your efforts as described. Large audiences mean you can set your own rate for working with brands.
- Start an Instagram business account and, depending on how often you post and your ability to persevere, have a business or an extra stream of income within two years.

Not long ago, a friend of a friend in the fashion/lifestyle industry set up an Instagram account purely to post little-seen photographs of Kate Moss. "Wheresmossy" has seen huge success and today boasts 56k followers. **Having an Instagram account with a large audience not only eases your pathway to earning money from affiliate marketing or advertising but can net you a job interview or clinch a job offer.** Young people, with engaged audiences, who are just branching into the field of influencer marketing may start by charging US\$25–50 per post. Established accounts (50–80k + followers) charge hundreds of dollars per post. If you're passionate about something, why not give it a try? Remember the 2Cs: content and consistency.

68

CHAPTER 6
SOCIAL MEDIA MANAGEMENT

HOW, HAVING BEEN MADE REDUNDANT SEVERAL TIMES, CORINNA ESSA TURNED HER ATTENTION ONLINE, HARNESSING THE POWER OF THE INTERNET TO FOUND HER OWN SOCIAL MEDIA MARKETING COMPANY.

From her early days in TV and media in London, Greece and France, Corinna was accustomed to working twelve-to-sixteen-hour days. Armed with three languages, a university degree and a few years of work experience, she was content to put the hours in to get where she wanted. But Corinna's story didn't go as smoothly as you'd imagine. She ploughed on until 2009 when the financial crisis hit Greece very hard. Even with all her qualifications, she could not find a job. Corinna was lucky to be mentored throughout her experience by her brother, himself a successful business owner, becoming an early adopter of online marketing. Through him, **she learned the power of the internet to create your own economy, to generate income streams regardless of geography and irrespective of whether you leave the house or not.** Today she is the owner of Social Media Worldwide, a social media marketing agency and is an author and a TEDx speaker with 35,000 fans on Facebook and 15,000 subscribers on YouTube. She is booked by companies around the world to speak at conferences and coach business leaders and entrepreneurs to leverage the power of social media to grow their online business. Corinna is on a personal quest to engage and educate people about the power of social media to amplify businesses.

Sound familiar? Corinna's story is similar to that of thousands of others. Either you've found it impossible to get a job post-education, or you've lost a job during the Covid-19 outbreak, had your salary slashed or can't get work experience no matter how hard you try. Corinna features in this book because she's overcome a lot of challenges to get to the enviable position she is in as I write. HER SUCCESS CAME ABOUT BECAUSE OF HER ATTITUDE TO CHANGE. As human beings we have a bad track record regarding change, preferring to act like it's not actually happening. Rather than burying her head in the sand, Corinna shook herself off and decided to tackle the work problem head on. She began to study her environment closely, saw the opportunities in the fledgling digital economy and launched herself into learning everything she possibly could about this new way of working and earning. She saw the opportunity and she seized it. Check Corinna out here: https://www.socialmediaworldwide.com/blog/author/corinna/

Back to the UK and it's February 2020, Laurence Moss was in revision mode for his GCSE exams when Covid-19 struck. The exams were cancelled leaving Laurence and his classmates very anxious about the future. But unlike his classmates, Laurence had quite enough to keep him busy.

> HOW LAURENCE MOSS LAUNCHED A FULL-SERVICE INSTAGRAM MARKETING AGENCY WHICH GREW FROM CONTENT HE GATHERED AS A HOBBY WHEN HE WAS THIRTEEN YEARS OLD.

At the age of thirteen Laurence Moss would play with getting posts to go viral on Instagram and collect likes for the pure fun of it! He wasn't focused on the marketing aspect until established eCommerce brands started to approach him offering him $50 at a time to post a photo on his Instagram account. By then he had grown an Instagram following of over 350k people across niches including memes, football, cars, animals and travel. By the following year he was providing Instagram-specific marketing consultancy services to big name brands and in 2019, at the age of fourteen, he created his Instagram marketing agency Greedy Growth. His first client was one of the largest pop culture auction companies in the US (https://www.forbes.com/sites/alisoncoleman/2020/06/07/how-this-teenage-entrepreneur-defied-the-bullies-and-grew-a-successful-business/). It's commonplace for companies to simply not have the time to learn and implement the social media strategies which could

leverage their businesses. Brands are all too willing to buy sponsored posts to reach numbers like the 350k followers which Laurence built up on Instagram communities. He has been steadily growing the business throughout the last nine months with a projected revenue of £4k per month by end of year. He runs his company alone although he calls on a remote team of freelancers, via Upwork, who deal with specific areas of his clients' projects when he's struggling to juggle school and work. Check Laurence out here:
https://greedygrowth.co.uk.

Social media marketers are responsible for managing a company's profile on social media sites like Twitter, Facebook and Instagram to build authority and bring them as many customers as possible. This might include creating content for posts, blogging and responding to questions or comments online. You will need to write well and be able to connect with customers which requires a high level of communication skills. Whilst social media in its infancy was mostly for fun, today it's a critical part of how everyone gets work done. From businesses to governments, social media is playing a critical part in discovering trends, enhancing brands, connecting with audiences and drawing traffic and attention to your work. The last ten years have seen a significant rise in the number of people choosing social media as a career option in a space that is ripe with opportunity. As with most skillsets, there are people with an innate understanding of these tools and how to use them and those that don't. **If you feel that you are particularly skilled at writing, communicating, engaging and anticipating trends, it would be worth approaching a social media agency to see if you could put**

your talent to use and get paid for it. It's not uncommon for successful young social media marketers to make up to 6 figures per year. If earning money from specialising in social media rocks your boat, think about investing your time and money in developing skills in any of the following four areas of expertise.

Four Areas in which to Build a Career as a Social Media Manager

<u>Content</u>
Along with anyone selling services or products on social media, brands need to have great content. For brands great content means offering value to consumers in the form of helping them, informing them, saving them money, offering them inspiration or entertainment. Today many brands are fighting to be featured in the social media streams of users who are offering value to their followers. **If you want to ace a career in social media, understanding content and how it works differently on different social platforms is critical.**

<u>Data</u>
This is a sure job for the future. **Entire careers will be built on understanding the data of social media.** Analytics that help you track the performance of your social media content provide invaluable information for business owners. This is a complex, exciting field in social for any of you with the curiosity and inclination to explore this further.

<u>Service</u>

Customer service is not new and continues to be critical for brands. As social media becomes ever more integrated into the consumer experience, companies need to increase their social listening to provide great customer service. **If you're a good listener, have skills in one-to-one communication and can read social situations well, then why not consider a career as a social media manager?**

<u>Advertising</u>

According to Carrie Kerpen, CEO of Likeable Media, an award-winning digital agency, social advertising is qualitatively different from traditional and even digital advertising. **Finding innovative social ad solutions requires a deep understanding of social behaviour that goes beyond re-targeting platforms.** Carrie considers that the person who becomes an expert in the placement, optimisation and reporting of social ads will have a key role in this industry going forward.

<u>What you might do as social media manager</u>

- Help businesses and entrepreneurs leverage the power of social media to sell their products and services;
- Create a strategic social media marketing plan for a business;
- Choose the right platform for that business. Not all platforms suit all businesses;

- Put together a content plan for the client, choosing the right voice and tone for the social media posts depending on the nature of the business.

The tasks involved mainly include content creation, audience engagement, curation, emails, outreach, reputation management, monitoring, performance tracking and a lot of scheduling. Analytics forms a large part of social media management to calculate key performance indicators like engagement rate, revenue and brand positioning. Social results would be measured and added to spreadsheets. Other key areas include checking in on and keeping up with eCommerce sales, influencers and, if you are positioning brands in different geographical areas, responding to and engaging with Asian, American or European markets.

If you want to use social media to market your own products on Instagram or eCommerce, follow the seven steps below to get a return on investment.

- Identify your goals
- Identify your audience
- Select the best platforms
- Remember the 2Cs: content and consistency
- Engage with influencers
- Grow your audience
- Engage your audience

Next steps if this is for you

There are plenty of social media programmes online but be aware that employers are seeking real-world experience much of the time. Social media changes quickly so there could be an advantage in learning on the job as an intern, instead of doing a course that may already be outdated by some months by the time you hit the market. Be aware that with this type of work you will need to be available for large parts of the day since part of having a good social media presence is responding to online questions and concerns as quickly as possible to meet customer demands. **Knowing the foundations of social media management is a starting point but you will need to stay on top of ever-shifting trends to become and remain a successful social media marketer.** Your profile should reflect your goals and should serve as a showcase of what a client can get if they hire you. Create profiles on Twitter, Facebook, Instagram and Fledglink. It's recommended that you master these platforms first. You can search for jobs online on Monster and Upwork. In the UK check out www.workinstartups.com.

Standout social media marketers persevere and put out content week in, week out, year after year. Laurence's advice to young people starting out is to "visualise what you want to build and work towards it. If you hit a roadblock, persevere and work it out and surround yourself with people on a similar journey to yours" (A. Coleman, "How this teenage entrepreneur defied the bullies and grew a successful business", www.forbes.com, June 7, 2020.)

Acknowledge that change is not comfortable. For anyone. It created discomfort for Corinna and Laurence too but they leaned into the discomfort and adapted to the environment.

CHAPTER 7
TWITTER

HOW A YOUNG, CREATIVE STYLE ICON FROM NEW YORK BECAME ONE OF THE MOST PERSUASIVE INFLUENCERS ON TWITTER.

If you're aged eighteen to twenty-five and want to know exactly what to wear, how to wear it, where to be seen and with whom, Luka Sabbat has the answer. With 404k followers on Twitter (check out @whoisluka), this cool fashionista with his suave good looks and sartorial flair has big name brands fighting for him to showcase their products. (https://www.inc.com/ian-jackson/social-media-teenage-allstars-13-of-todays-rising-stars.html). He's worked with some of the biggest brands in the world including American Eagle and Tommy Hilfiger, has launched exhibitions of his own and has won various accolades along the way including being nominated for the Shorty Award in recognition of individuals producing great content across all the media channels.

Luka is featured in the book because **his social media skills are the envy of advertisers everywhere, generating such a level of fervid engagement from his fanbase that there are thousands of likes on every post.** Interestingly, Luka's metrics are relatively modest (compared to a fanbase of 20m for example) but his influence is enormous. As I've said previously, don't get caught up in the numbers. If your followers hang on to your every word and trust you to make recommendations, brands seek you out precisely because of your close links to the consumers of their products.

<u>Twitter as an income source</u>
Although this platform doesn't attract as many teenagers as it did at the turn of the century, Twitter still offers great opportunities for earning a living. Best known for news-breaking tweets from celebrities and politicians, the platform is freely used by businesses and individuals alike. It's as much about getting to know what's happening in the world and sharing your opinion about it, as it is about business and brands. But for many young people, Twitter is about brands and, put simply, money. Once you create an account, you can create posts of up to 280 characters (up from the traditional 140-character tweets) and tweet any number of times throughout the day (your tweets will be distributed to followers in a feed).

To make money on Twitter you'll need a great Twitter profile and you'll need to grow your followers. For the profile, it's important to have a branded look on the platform including a professional profile photo, a Twitter cover photo, a matching username and a description of what you do. After that, it's a matter of posting regular content and engaging with other Twitter users in your niche. Follow people relevant to your industry. Promote your Twitter profile on other social media platforms, embed your Twitter feed in your website and like, retweet and comment on other users' tweets for engagement (https://optinmonster.com/make-money-on-twitter/).

Promoting a product on Twitter is straightforward. You simply publish a tweet. Plan your strategy first. What products will you promote and how does that product relate to you? For example, if you have a large Twitter following and play sport at county or national level, you may choose to promote a health drink that you regularly consume during training. Your strategy document should include elements such as: what you want to achieve by promoting this particular product, what messages you're putting out there, how the message aligns with your values, which hashtags you will use (using the right hashtags will ensure you'll show up for users searching for health food drinks). This will help to tighten your message each time you tweet. You might post a tweet with a great photo of the health drink, an engaging description of the product and why you love it, include a hashtag (so users looking for health drinks can find you) and a link to the website of the drink manufacturer. As an affiliate or depending on the kind of agreement you have with the product owner, you will get paid every time someone buys that health drink via your Twitter account.

Monetising your Twitter account

<u>Affiliate marketing</u>
Affiliate marketing has long been associated with promoting products in blogs or on websites, but you can earn decent money promoting affiliate products on Twitter. If you have a solid presence on the platform and a large following, you can monetise your Twitter account by signing up for affiliate programmes (such as Amazon's affiliate programme) and promoting other people's products. You earn a commission on every sale that you bring in for the company. You do this by directing your followers to their site. If they buy via the link you shared on your Twitter account, you get paid. In general, you'll need to have 5,000 followers at a minimum (this is the magic figure most often used as a basic benchmark) but it is possible to do sponsored tweets in certain niche areas with less than 100 followers and a mere 100 posts.

If you tweet about products or services using your affiliate link and your followers click the link and purchase, you'll earn money for directing them to the site. Again, choose ads carefully. If you promote a dozen different products, your followers will lose trust in your voice and won't act on your recommendations. You can choose products from a huge selection of affiliate categories from business or investing to education and from games to e-business and e-marketing. **Promote high-quality products in your niche that you would consider purchasing or have bought yourself.** Remember you're in the business of offering value to your followers. Your audience trusts your recommendations and is more likely to buy something that you've tried and liked. Only 10% to 20% of your tweets should include affiliate links; the rest should be engaging content. The more authentic you are the better you will do.

Sponsored tweets

If you're a regular tweeter with an online presence, companies will pay you to tweet about their services, products and brand. Find out about this on www.sponsoredTweets.com, a platform which connects you to companies that will pay for tweets. On the platform, you can choose from a list of ads to tweet about. There's no reason not to do this. If you're already a big Twitter user, you may as well earn money by doing something you normally do for free. Choose ads carefully, ensuring they suit your niche or niches and that your values align with the sponsors of the ad. If you're tweeting your own stuff on the side and it doesn't resonate with your sponsor, it's not authentic and you may lose the relationship with the sponsor. We know that employees have been fired for what they tweet and it's no different with a sponsor. Cultivate your business relationships whatever they may be. Brands that pay for sponsored tweets want maximum exposure which means you'll need a sizeable following. Typically, you'll earn a flat fee for tweeting about a product or service. If you have a large dedicated following, you can approach brands you love and offer to promote their product to your followers by sending a personal message in exchange for a fee. You can schedule tweets using applications like Hootsuite.

MyLikes

www.mylikes.com is another social media ad platform that can be used on Twitter (or on your blog or YouTube channel). It connects you to companies looking to pay for tweets. You get paid up to 42 cents per click on ads you tweet for other people. You choose an ad (or ads) from literally thousands of sponsors on the platform and you get to schedule when the ad will be tweeted from your Twitter account.

Paid per Tweet

www.paidpertweet.com allows companies to access millions of Twitter users whom they pay to promote their product, service or brand. It used to be that only influencers with hundreds of thousands of followers were approached by large companies. Today nano- and micro-influencers are increasingly targeted by big companies and, in niche areas, Twitter users are approached with as little as 50 dedicated followers.

Innovate to make money on Twitter

Design an app for fellow Twitter users. Jon Negroni from @lifehack suggests watching your audience carefully to figure out what they need e.g. this might be an app that lets you generate hashtags automatically, based on popularity. It may already exist as things move fast in this environment!

Build followers for someone else's Twitter account

Another great way to earn money is to build followers for someone else's Twitter account. Use websites like Fiverr to promote your business (Google search descriptors like "We build followers on Twitter" to help you to draw up your business profile) and charge people for building their accounts. Jon Negroni at Lifehack says that he did this himself at one point earning five dollars for every 100 followers gained for a client.

Earn money on Twitter from Ad.ly

www.adly.com is another ad service but instead of getting paid per click you create a profile of your interests on this platform (much like making a bid for consultancy work in the offline world) and advertisers can choose your Twitter account to publicise their campaign. You agree to send out x number of tweets and you get paid a lump sum much like you would a piece of consultancy work.

<u>Copywriting</u>
We've spoken a lot about writing being a superpower in this book! Twitter is a marvellous showcase for your language and grammar skills. If you can craft beautifully worded, engaging tweets that can promote or sell anything in 280 characters, why not get yourself hired to write for a living. Search "social media" on job boards to find advertisements such as "Develop, write and edit marketing and communications materials on Twitter and Facebook for our client". Bingo!

<u>Arrange a Twitter contest</u>
If you know of a business that wants to gain more publicity, you could link up with them, offer to arrange a Twitter contest and negotiate a fee based on the sales that come in. Nothing engages people more than a prize. There are all sorts of ways to make a contest enticing for followers. They can be judges or you can ask them for ideas or simply get them to retweet or favourite something in return for a prize. For example, you could promote a contest or giveaway such as "RT We're giving away a pack of 12 DrinksUp Energy Drinks. Simply RT + Follow to enter. The contest closes at midnight on Thursday. Must be following. Winners announced Friday. Hashtags". Including calls to actions builds your following and can generate sales over time.

<u>Using Twitter to sell your own products</u>
If you have your own product, Twitter is a great way to make money. You keep all the profit and you're in the driving seat. Your followers are already following you

because they like what you do, so you have a customer fan base. You can find other customers too (not your existing followers) based on Twitter bios using Twitter's search engine tool. This is an amazing advantage because you can simply search for "where to buy a supersized paddling pool" and then tweet the people who come up in the resulting feed and let them know you're promoting supersized paddling pools. One of the most successful strategies is to use discounts (the old-fashioned way) and promotions to spur spending. A limited time sale will attract customers to your site, and by selling from Twitter, you can reach people around the world and send them to your website rather than just targeting people who visit your website. Be careful not to overwhelm your Twitter feed with too much selling.

You can also create Twitter ads to promote your product. These will appear in the feed marked "Promoted" or "Sponsored". Just like on Facebook, you can promote your ad to users based on their interests, demographics and activity on Twitter.

<u>Editing</u>
Again, if you've proved yourself to be a whizz on Twitter, this is a great proof of concept for your writing skills and you can easily sell an ability to craft the written word to a company who outsource their social media. Writing a couple of posts every day on two or three social media platforms is extremely time-consuming for companies most of whom outsource the work to agencies. If writing English or French or Spanish or Chinese is your thing, check out companies online that are doing a really bad job of their social media marketing and approach them directly.

<u>Find out what your followers want and produce it for them</u>
My teen is a massive fan of fantasy author Neil Gaiman, who became famous for "A Calendar of Tales". Interestingly the content for this creation came from Neil's large Twitter audience whom he asked to submit questions to him. The short stories came about as he answered questions posed by fans. How clever is that? Find out what your audience is looking for and cater to them.

<u>Twitter Media Studio</u>
This is a bit more advanced but is a useful tool for monetising your Twitter account. Alison Hott writing for OptinMonster, suggests using Twitter Media Studio on the platform which works in the same way as placing ads in your videos and live streams on YouTube to make money from advertisers. Using Twitter Media Studio, you can place in-stream video ads and video sponsorships in your Twitter videos so you can earn money directly from advertisers on the platform.

<u>Twittad</u>
This network www.twittads.com is an ethical, transparent platform that allows you to bid to do sponsored tweets. You set up your own cost-per-click and see if advertisers will accept your bid. Make sure that you identify your niche so advertisers/sponsors can align themselves with your product or service. If they choose you, you will send out specific, pre-set Tweets from their publicity campaign from your account.

Next steps if this is for you
The secret on Twitter is simply to be active. At the least, create an account today and start tweeting. Even if

you don't have a product to sell, you can use Twitter to send people to your website (or your client's website) so they can read a blog post or find the latest recipe e.g. sharing a blog post on Twitter will grow your audience and your blogging career and boost numbers to your website. When you publish a new article for your blog, it costs nothing to create a tweet about the article which will drive people from Twitter back to your blog. It generates traffic for your site, blog or eCommerce business in the same way as creating a pin for a new article drives traffic from Pinterest to your website, blog or shop.

CHAPTER 8
TIKTOK

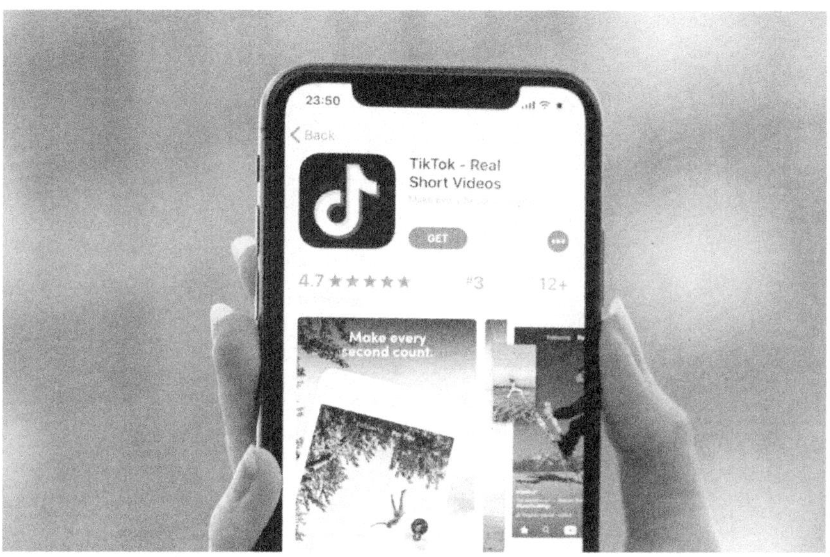

HOW ONE UNASSUMING TEEN BECAME THE HIGHEST EARNING TIKTOK USER IN THE UK AND A SOCIAL MEDIA PHENOMENON.

Holly Hubert Horne, twenty-four, from Guernsey in the UK, grew up dreaming of being in musicals and took dance lessons until she was sixteen. She was an early adaptor of Vine and Musical.ly, which later became TikTok, and on the platform she is quite literally a superstar. She is provided with bodyguards when she attends events, has fans flying from all over the world to see her and her appearance at a shopping mall on a Saturday would close the place down (L. France, "Is TikTok star Holly H the most influential 23-year-old in Britain?", www.thetimes.co.uk, 2 Nov, 2019). Her influence is such that as of August 2020, she has 16.6m followers on TikTok, 1.5m followers on Instagram and 371k subscribers on YouTube. Holly is estimated to earn £60k for each fifteen-second sponsored post to her 16m followers. She also has a line in casual wear, with merchandise such as leggings and hoodies that sport the slogan 'professional weirdo'. She's worked with Disney, Pretty Little Thing, Warner Bros, Nickelodeon, Unilever and CBBC amongst others. Check out @hollyh for more information.

Holly had done her A-levels and had a place lined up at university, when she decided to convince her Mum to give her time to turn Holly H into a career. She negotiated one year's grace to make it work and began posting videos every single day, at the end of which she had amassed 110k followers but hadn't yet made any money. She was still convinced that this could become a career and ploughed on.

TikTok is the Chinese micro-video platform that resulted from the merger of the Chinese app Douyin with the lip-syncing app Musical.ly. This social network for young creators and aspiring influencers was launched in 2016 by its Chinese tech entrepreneur owner, Zhang Yiming and by October 2020 the app had surpassed 2 billion mobile downloads worldwide. Given that it was born of two apps steeped in music, central to the TikTok concept is the soundtrack, many going viral and becoming mainstream hits. Songs are regarded as key to the success of influencer campaigns on this platform. Already this has led to a change in the way that music producers create songs, many writing snippets of songs that lend themselves to the app and only producing the whole song if it's picked up on TikTok. Culturally the app is changing not only the way music is produced but how a generation of sixteen to twenty-four-year-olds dresses, dances, jokes and poses. TikTok is said to be ahead of competitors in how it uses AI, with powerful algorithms tracking user behaviour so that it offers you a continual stream of videos optimised for what you like.

In early 2019, few people were making real money on TikTok, the main perks at the time being high viewer numbers and lots of likes, but all of that has changed. Brands have started to descend on an app that gets two billion sets of eyes scrolling through it regularly. TikTok stars have the power to shift products and big brands want in. By the end of 2019, major brands like MAC and ELF Cosmetics had run campaigns on the platform and TikTok sensations like Holly H were starting to earn multiple millions of US dollars on the platform.

Monetising your TikTok account

<u>Be clear about your brand</u>
How do you want your followers to see you? What messages do you want to give to companies who are looking for influencers? Decide who you are and who will love your product (your target market and your target brands) and create the videos especially for them. Are you posting pranks? Are your videos funny or cool? What's your thing?

<u>Great Content</u>
Whether you're a social influencer on TikTok, YouTube, Twitter or Instagram, content is key. Posting new material requires a constantly fresh perspective, an understanding of your target audience and knowledge of the latest dance trends and current challenges. Content needs to be quirky, authentic and interesting and comic videos seem to perform better on this platform.

Attract followers
The best way to do this is to understand what your target market wants to see and give them content multiple times a day. Like Holly, if you're posting bite-sized videos with funny, entertaining or interesting content daily, you will draw an audience to you. Your audience should be able to identify with you. When Holly is asked why she's so successful on the platform, she freely admits that it's really hard to define. She does believe that being authentic and being in the moment is what people respond to remarking that "A lot of the stuff that is very natural is the stuff people respond to the best". You don't have to have a follower count like Holly's for brands to approach you. You've seen in previous chapters that influencers with dedicated, highly engaged audiences are approached with as little as 1k followers. In specialised, high-value niches even lower.

Sponsored Posts
Once you've amassed enough followers (at least 1k) you can start to earn money. Influencers can shift products like nothing else and branding deals follow the traction. Successful influencers are choosy about the products they endorse and open with their followers if they're being paid to advertise something. Young audiences are media-savvy, they know what paid content is. Check out Loren Gray who creates content for Revlon's TikTok account and posts Revlon-sponsored content on her own account. Loren has 45m followers and reportedly nets about US$42,000 per post.

Personal merchandise
If you're a successful Tiktoker, you could delve into entrepreneurship, creating your own line of makeup

products or fashion accessories. Lisa and Lena, identical twins from Stuttgart, were the first Tiktokers to build a lucrative empire with modelling careers, a clothing line and a pop hit. They have since quit TikTok to cater to an older audience but blazed a trail for influencers like Holly to branch into merchandising, amongst other businesses.

<u>Influencer marketing</u>
As a TikTok influencer, a company might hire you to create videos that promote their products, services or brand in order to generate sales. The influencers that a company hires are given a brief to follow e.g. one of the big influencer promotional campaigns on TikTok was for Mucinex cough medicine. Influencers were told to watch a zombie dance and record and upload their version of the dance on video, with the hashtag BeatTheZombieFunk. The idea behind the campaign is that with Mucinex, you can avoid that dreaded zombie feeling you get when you're ill! The hashtag challenge was downloaded 738 million times, generating massive engagement for the brand. Brands like Mucinex are putting a lot of effort into improving their campaigns with the help of influencers and creative agencies. Another campaign was for the rebooted Charlie's Angels movie. The campaign involved fifteen influencers performing a dance or skit to the lead single on the film's soundtrack "Don't Call me Angel".
Placing ads on TikTok is expensive compared to other platforms. It does offer several options for advertisers to reach their target audience. First off, you must have a TikTok advertising account or account manager. You submit information to TikTok and if you qualify, someone will get in touch with you to set up your advertising account. There are different types of ads such as:

In-Feed Video. The ad appears in the native news feed of TikTok on the For You page.

Brand Takeover. The ad appears when you open the app and fills the screen momentarily before becoming an In-Feed Video ad.

Hashtag Challenge. This is the ad format used by Mucinex for their "Beat the Zombie Funk Campaign". The ad appears on the Discovery page, encouraging users to compete in challenges to create the best digital content.

Branded AR Content. The ad appears as branded lenses, stickers, and other two-dimensional and three-dimensional content, as well as augmented reality content, for you to use in your videos.

Custom Influencer Package. The ad appears as part of sponsored content created by a TikTok influencer.

Check out Kristi Hines on Hootsuite for more information about TikTok advertising.

<u>Launch other careers from your influencer status</u>
Once you become TikTok famous, you can use your fame to launch a career as an actress or as a music artist. You can also launch yourself across different platforms e.g. Holly H also has a YouTube channel with 4m views, which means she earns money from ads on YouTube as well as TikTok.

<u>Become a TikTok consultant</u>
You can make money across all the social media platforms by transforming yourself into an expert on the platform and selling your services as a consultant. There is scope for work from experts in a host of different areas.

Companies and celebrities will happily pay for young, media–savvy people with business intellect, to draw up a strategy, create content, build a brand, get some excitement going and boost followers. There are plenty of businesses and celebrities! in need of help and willing to pay a TikTok Consultant to run their pages. Check out the social media of companies you know. Is it good? Are they getting traction? Does anything look strange e.g. millions of followers on one platform and little traction on another? Celebrities often use TikTok to coincide with global film releases, particularly as TikTok is so big in China and India. This platform is definitely the place for a global audience and if you have expertise on TikTok it can be monetised.

Read on to discover how one young man is earning in excess of US$10k per month as a consultant, helping companies and celebrities build their presence on TikTok.

https://www.vox.com/the-goods/2020/3/6/21155067/how-to-make-money-on-tiktok-consultant-seansaucetv

HOW A YOUNG AMERICAN WENT VIRAL ON TIKTOK WITH HIS HIGHLY PRODUCED PRANK VIDEOS.

Sean Young @seansaucetv is a twenty-seven-year-old American with over 1m followers on TikTok. Like Holly, Sean was already big on Vine (a precursor to Tik Tok which closed down in 2016) when he signed up to TikTok, quickly going viral with his signature videos.

Much of his earnings however come from working as a consultant to clients keen to use his expertise to get on the app. The million-plus followers on his own account serves as a calling card, lending him credibility when he pitches to clients. By the end of 2019, Sean was being approached by big brand names and celebrities all of them looking to launch on TikTok. Very few people, within their own marketing teams, specialised in this newest platform. Sean quickly became known as The TikTok Guy! In 2019, Sean was earning in the region of US$200k per year, much of it from his work for brands. He does song deals with some of the musicians he works with, earns money from his work with America's Funniest Home Videos and boasts several celebrities on his client books. Check out Rebecca Jennings' interview with Sean Young on this link:

https://www.vox.com/the-goods/2020/3/6/21155067/how-to-make-money-on-tiktok-consultant-seansaucetv.

Next steps if this is for you

Bear in mind that the audience is young. The "For You" page on TikTok caters towards kids so you will have to balance being PG but funny at the same time, to cater to the wider audience on the app. Post content appropriate for the app. In other words, put your message across in a way that's appropriate to TikTok. If that means doing a funny dance, so be it. Your fans will love it.

The secret is to create content that doesn't require language or dialogue but sounds and music. The quirkier the video, the more you get reposted to potentially become a meme. Remember that the life span of videos is about two days, so you will have to plan out content and shoot lots of videos together to have enough material.

If you enjoy being in front of the camera and like the process of shooting short videos of yourself or of other people, spend a few months learning every aspect of TikTok and sell your expertise. Laurence Moss did precisely this on Instagram. He delved deep into the Instagram algorithm, learning everything he possibly could about how it works and established a business to help people optimise their Instagram accounts. Offer to consult to companies or influencers by helping them to shoot videos and source music and generally build the brand (see consultancy above). Write a description of what you do on a work–for–hire platform, offer to run campaigns for brands, get into the TikTok marketing wing of companies, Offer your services as an intern to TikTok Superstars. For anyone looking for revenue streams, there is a lot of potential in a social app that is growing as quickly as TikTok.

96

CHAPTER 9
ENTREPRENEURSHIP

HOW THIS AWARD-WINNING, YOUNG TECH ENTREPRENEUR AGREED A MULTI-MILLION-POUND MERGER DEAL AT EIGHTEEN YEARS OLD.

Ben Towers, at twenty-two years old, is generally acknowledged as an entrepreneurial force. When he was eleven, one of his family members challenged him to design a website and that was the start of what would become Towers Design, a marketing company employing twenty-two people with big-name clients like Twitter! Although it started out as a bit of fun, by the time he was thirteen Ben realised the business potential after a conversation with his grandfather (https://www.greatbritishentrepreneurawards.com/news/self-starter-ben-towers/). Passionate about his projects, whilst still at school he employed freelancers to help him grow his business, employing himself as an apprentice in his own firm after completing his GCSEs!! In 2016 he won the NatWest Young Entrepreneur of the Year Award and in 2017, aged just eighteen, Towers Design was merged with Zest The Agency in a multi-million-pound deal, with Ben subsequently exiting the business. He went on to co-found Tahora, a social platform aimed at helping employees feel more engaged, connected and productive at work through an improved sense of community and wellbeing. He consults to leading brands and gives keynote addresses at conferences around the world. Richard Branson refers to Ben as one of the UK's most exciting entrepreneurs. Check Ben out here: https://bentowers.com.

If none of the alternatives in previous chapters strike you as the way forward with your career, perhaps starting your own business is something you would consider. Throughout this book we've seen young entrepreneurs take on the business world. Being your own boss will come with its challenges but as evidenced by these young people, it can also offer freedom and a deep sense of satisfaction in creating something of your own. Entrepreneurship is not for the faint-hearted. It comes with its own risks and of course, there's a danger that your business doesn't succeed (if it happened to Richard Branson, it can happen to you!). But if you're an acute observer of the world, can see problems which you feel you can solve with a great business idea, are highly motivated and enthusiastic, then this is a path you could pursue.

Entrepreneurs learn to reframe problems and notably are willing to take a risk. For entrepreneurs, problems represent opportunity. Apple Crider believes that entrepreneurship is all about solving problems. One of the first things to do to develop the mindset of an entrepreneur is to start to see the problems faced by the customers you serve. Observe the problem, then consider how you can solve it. Lachlan Delchau-Jones and Taylor Reilly did precisely that when they anticipated that whole families being forced to stay indoors together in lockdown required a solution for boredom, anxiousness and overcrowding!

Michael Hyatt, author and coach, believes that entrepreneurs are very good for society because they're curious and motivated to solve problems whether for financial rewards or personal or altruistic reasons. Whether in education, health, data science, in the military or the non-profit world, solving problems benefits the whole of society. Entrepreneurship offers a wealth of opportunity, but it can be an obstacle-strewn road and, for the most part, success is some way into the future. It offers a viable route for those hungry for success but **the life of an entrepreneur, whilst exciting and rewarding, is not for the risk averse. If you value security and certainty entrepreneurship may not be for you.** In reality, if you have to examine whether you could adapt to the life of an entrepreneur in your teens, then it's not for you…. not yet. I say not yet because there are many instances of people becoming very successful entrepreneurs later, once they find the problem they want to solve. You could start your journey into entrepreneurship slowly by securing an internship and/or working in a startup to learn from the bottom up. Working in a startup not only offers you highly relevant experience but exposes you to roles and responsibilities which would not be available in established companies. There isn't a right or a wrong way to do this.

One young man who is motivated to solve problems is Brendan Cox, a twenty-year-old serial entrepreneur from New Jersey whose goal is to raise the quality of branding, especially in small businesses, and to ensure that entrepreneurs have the resources they need to develop large, successful ventures. Brendan has established various businesses, specialising in graphic design and branding, including Cox Visuals, Teen Assistant and Business Blurb. Once again, we meet an entrepreneur with a desire to pay it forward and to help solve problems through his business.

HOW BRENDAN COX' PASSION TO HELP SMALL BUSINESSES LED TO HIM PIONEERING THE FUTURE OF BUSINESS THROUGH HIS MEDIA COMPANY, BUSINESS BLURB.

In a recent interview with Mary Juetten for Forbes Online Magazine https://www.forbes.com/sites/maryjuetten/2020/06/04/ten-tips-for-success-from-a-teen-entrepreneur/, Brendan offered the following tips for early-stage entrepreneurs and founders:-

1. **"Action Over Words**: Take action and stop spending months perfecting every little detail on your business plan. Jump in and learn as you go. One of the perks of being a young entrepreneur is that your life doesn't depend on the success of this company. Talk is cheap. It's easy to make it look like you're doing a lot when really all you're really doing is talking about the things you want to do. A lot of people start businesses without planning any proper course of action, and things

tend to fall apart. You need to know exactly how you're going to make something happen before you tell people you're going to do it. Customers lose confidence in businesses that talk but never act.

2. **Set Realistic Goals**: Setting goals is one thing but setting realistic goals is something different entirely. Your goals need to be challenging but still accomplishable. People tell me every day that they want to go from 0 to 100,000 followers on Instagram in a week but it's not realistic.

3. **Don't Start a Business to Make Money:** Yes, I know that phrase sounds extremely contradictory. What I mean by this is to start a business doing what you love and are passionate about. Don't start a business with the sole purpose of making money because you will lose interest very quickly and the business will flop.

4. **Connections are Key:** I can't stress this enough. Connections are everything in business. In the business world, it's all about who you know not what you know. Build a network of people for everything so that way you have a person for everything.

5. **Social Media is Everything**: If your business isn't on social media, you barely have a business these days. Think of social media as a way to share your business among millions of unique users daily. Use social media to your advantage when it comes to marketing your business and creating an image for your brand.

6. **Don't Be Afraid to Fail:** Failure sucks, don't get me wrong. I lost US$10,000 in 8th grade after investing in an account to build a targeted Instagram brand. Then one day, the platform suddenly deleted the account. There's no point in

keeping your head down, use your failures to motivate you to succeed more. Capitalize on what you learned from failure.

7. **You Don't Know It All**: Education is a life-long process, nobody knows everything. You should always be willing to take advice and listen to others. Platforms and the business world are always changing. No matter the age or experience, listen to that person's advice and then apply it to your knowledge and business so you can continue to expand and adjust.

8. **Understand Competitive Value**: Use your competitors as motivation. Allow them to push you to improve your company and your skillset. But don't become obsessed. Understand the value of competition and use it to focus more on your company. Don't get sidetracked by your goals, while staring at someone else who is achieving new heights.

9. **Believe in Yourself**: Stop second-guessing every decision you make. Just because it hasn't been done, doesn't mean it won't succeed. When running a business, you are going to make mistakes whether large or small. It's okay and it's part of the process. You can do it, so stop telling yourself you can't.

10. **Don't Be Afraid to Re-Invest**: Many companies stop growing because they become comfortable with a steady revenue. However, if you want to grow, you need to re-invest in yourself and your company. It's okay not to make a profit overnight. Success takes time and you need to be willing to understand that."

Check Brendan out here: https://www.brendanacox.com.

I included Brendan's tips because he offers such good advice for entrepreneurs but also because it's cutting edge, coming as it does from a young, serial entrepreneur who is in the thick of the action right now. My thanks to Mary Juetten for the kind permission to reprint this content from her interview with Brendan.

Whilst Brendan was pioneering the future of business on social media, another teenager, across the pond, was busy following her dreams. This young entrepreneur from Aberystwyth in Wales, had her eyes very firmly set on growing a business and was devoting all her energy to actioning her plans.

FROM A LOVE OF MAKING SWEET-TREATS TO WINNING THE APPRENTICE, HOW ALANA SPENCER'S ENTREPRENEURIAL PURSUITS LEAD TO A PARTNERSHIP WITH SIR ALAN SUGAR AND A BUSINESS THAT LIGHTS HER UP.

Alana Spencer got into business early, making cards with a friend at school when she was 9 years old. Not very motivated by academics, she did know from very early on that she wanted to grow a business. She set up her first company, creating luxury chocolates from a rented kitchen, aged 17 and from there moved on to cakes. From a love of making sweet–treats and a strong desire to succeed in business, Ridiculously Rich Cakes was born. In 2016 Alana appeared on The Apprentice going on to win the £250k investment prize and a partnership with Sir Alan Sugar. Today, with a team of ambassadors selling cakes across the country and a core group of people supporting her in the business, this young entrepreneur is scaling the heights and, at 25 years old, her journey is just beginning.

https://www.walesonline.co.uk/business/business-news/13-things-you-need-know-12338305.

Alana's advice for budding entrepreneurs:

1. Stop overthinking your ideas and just go for it! You won't know until you try and you can learn along the way.
2. It's really easy to get caught up in the creative and fun parts at the beginning of your business journey but, ultimately, it's the sales that are going to make and grow your business so don't neglect focusing on different ways to sell your product/service.

All three of the entrepreneurs in this chapter have a lot of energy, a clear direction and are persistent in their efforts to achieve their goals. All three are stretched beyond their limits. This brings us conveniently to the subject of outsourcing as a vital component of business for many young businesspeople. When there's a need, many entrepreneurs find freelancers to support them in moving their projects to where they want them to be. It's important to have this mindset if you're trying to grow a business and study or work at the same time.

<u>Rules for running a business if you're under 18</u>
Do check out the rules for running a business where you live. Are the annual tax allowance and liabilities the same for under eighteens as adults? Know your tax-free allowance and the rate at which you'll pay tax above that. Will you have to set yourself up as a sole trader? What's the maximum amount you can earn before you have to operate as a sole trader? How old must you be to be a director of a limited company? It's difficult to find funding if you're under eighteen although Nick d'Aloisio of Summly (which was bought out by Yahoo for $30m in

2013) managed to secure substantial seed money from Li Ka-shing (Hong Kong's billionaire investor) when he was still only sixteen years old. Most banks require a company director to be eighteen to open a business bank account but Monzo accepts applications from sixteen-year olds.

Next steps if this is for you

Where do you go next if you fancy yourself as the next Ben Towers, Alana Spencer or Brendan Cox? If you're dreaming of becoming your own boss and have an idea for a business, talk to someone about it. Brainstorm it with family, friends or someone at school. Many of the entrepreneurs I've spoken to throughout the book felt that entrepreneurship should be encouraged and celebrated as a subject at school. Read more about this on the Cosmikos blogpost www.cosmikos.com. Some reported feeling demotivated as teenagers by reactions to their business ideas. If you have an idea of a product or service for a business and are advised to get a degree or get work experience in that field first, consider the advice carefully. If you're confident about your idea, rather than become demotivated by the feedback, consider investigating ways of setting up on your own and doing those things for your own business. Consider how you might action that. Check out young entrepreneurship schemes (see below) and talk about your idea with more than one person.

If you're an entrepreneur-in-the-making, one crucial thing you will need is a network. Connecting to other entrepreneurs, sharing your ideas and offering each other support is vital. Most countries have government-backed initiatives that offer established routes to entrepreneurship for young entrepreneurs. Such schemes are highly sought after and provide training, mentoring, office space and introductions to other ambitious, young entrepreneurs.

Whatever country you're in, there are likely to be financial schemes that provide easy access to funds for startups and there are lots of grants. **Just google "government-backed schemes promoting new business" and "startup business grants" where you live** for further information. You may find a co-founder in these spaces or an invaluable mentor or contacts of a lifetime. You'll have to show that you have the ambition to build scalable businesses and convince the organisation that you're enterprising, creative and willing to take risks, but being accepted into these circles can be ground-breaking. Entrepreneurship is a long game with inherent risks. We hear about the successful businesses, not the startups that no longer exist. If your business is your passion, you're more likely to stick with it for the long haul.

A final word for anyone feeling slightly disappointed they don't have an idea for a business. Just because you don't fancy becoming an entrepreneur now doesn't mean it's not for you. **Many very successful entrepreneurs put in the hours learning the ropes with big brands before switching to entrepreneurship later. If it's on the cards for you, there's time for this to happen.**

CHAPTER 10
21st CENTURY JOBS

HOW ALICE PEARSON RESIGNED HER POSITION IN PR TO ESTABLISH A CAKE BUSINESS CALLED COPPER SPOON CAKERY.

Before setting up her cake business, Alice had a busy life in the city of Leeds. Her city job was stressful, and she would bake to unwind and relax. When she first moved into her PR role in the city, she started a blog in which she would write about baking. She would also bring her test-bakes into work and her colleagues loved them. At this point she realised that she could turn the blog into a business. She moved from the city to the countryside and set up her cake business working from home. Whilst occasionally she misses the city and her friends, her business has gone from strength to strength and easy access to the countryside has helped facilitate her work–life balance. For Alice, switching careers was the right move. In an interview with The Guardian newspaper she said, "I cannot tell you how rewarding it is to create a successful business out of something you love". Check out the Copper Spoon Cakery here: www.copperspooncakery.com (https://www.theguardian.com/money/2019/jun/01/all-change-how-to-leave-the-city-and-find-a-new-career.).

Career switching is becoming increasingly commonplace in the 2020s. Whilst you're unlikely to be thinking of a career switch as you kickstart your working life, it is reassuring to know that you can take on a job in PR and switch to writing or carving out your dream business later in the journey. Alice features in the book as a successful young businesswoman who had the courage and conviction to switch careers, made possible by online tools that help in the building and marketing of a business from scratch. This is a lovely example of how to live life on your own terms, availing of ways of working that were not possible twenty years ago. Finding personal fulfilment can happen at any age, in all circumstances. It is possible to make a comfortable living and live the dream without earning millions.

In the Deloitte Review (Issue 21), Josh Bersin asks you to imagine that you're a surfer. You gear up, educating yourself and upskilling, then armed with that knowledge, you catch a good wave early and ride it until it hits the beach and calms. Then you paddle out, observing the environment, upskilling and re-educating yourself and you start to look for the next wave. So, **your career is a series of waves. With each new wave, you gain new skills**

and experiences and continue to invest in personal development to keep up with the latest trends. This is a useful analogy to help you visualise investing in educating yourself to catch the next big opportunity (in eCommerce or Big Tech or the music industry). Whereas your grandfather or grandmother may have had one career (no surfing), your parents have probably had a couple of careers (surfing) and you will likely work multiple jobs simultaneously (see Chapter 11 on the Gig Economy) or have a working life characterised by half a dozen or more career switches.

Along with large corporates, there are thousands of smaller businesses that require your help now. Much of the available work is coming from successful online businesses which require digitally savvy videographers, content writers, marketers, designers, social media managers and a wide variety of job roles unheard of ten years ago. Jobs are changing, and if your mental job spec still revolves around legal secretary or printing and publishing roles (in the old-fashioned sense) then read on. The expertise most in demand by large multinationals in the 2020s include the following:

Expertise Required in 21st Century

Cloud computing	Nanotechnology
AI	Mobile app development
Security consultancy	Video and audio production
Data science	UX design
Analysis	SEO/SEM marketing (search
Sales leadership	engine optimisation / search

Translation

Physical therapy

Engineering

Medical science

Writing

Marketing

engine marketing)

Blockchain

Industrial design

Digital journalism

Animation

Implant organ designers

Whilst data science and technology-related degrees are a sure route to a career in the twenty-first century, there are some common misconceptions. You don't need a degree in Computer Science or tech to get a good job and, if you are interested in technology but don't want to attend university, there are plenty of ways to transition into tech without going to university. Whether through apprenticeships, live skills-based classes on Zoom, a Google Career Certificate★ (https://grow.google/certificates/) or Accredited Online Courses, you can train in skillsets that fit the market. Your career path will look clearer if you have a degree in one of the "topselling" areas of expertise but, as you've seen, there are lots of routes to finding paid work that can transform your earnings. Choose just one area that's in high demand in the market (from coding to writing content) and invest time, as Laurence Moss did, to learn everything about it.

★Google Career Certificates, hosted on Coursera, teach job-ready skills to kickstart your career. Designed by Google, courses such as IT Support, UX Design, Project Management and Data Analysis, are taught over a six-month period after which the certified person is connected directly to employers seeking these qualifications. Scholarships are available and the courses cost US$49 per month (£37 per month) for the duration of the course (usually six months). Someone with a UX Design qualification could expect to earn US$84k (£63k) per year entering the market.

Twenty-first century working life will be characterised by career switches or, for many, and we are beginning to see evidence of this, will comprise largely of many consultancy type assignments up to the equivalent of full-time hours. The challenge will be to anticipate the next assignment and research the education required to gain those skills. Consultants and entrepreneurs are used to working this way. Keeping ears to the ground, getting a feel for the market, anticipating trends, constantly selling themselves, defining and redefining their work and educating themselves to keep up with the latest thing. Today, everyone is expected to continuously learn and upskill. Whether you're working for a business, for yourself or for the State, (as a business owner, freelancer, influencer, teacher, doctor, lawyer, engineer or scientist), to be successful you have to be more entrepreneurial when thinking about and planning your life and your finances. And the most entrepreneurial people today are interested in passive income, the idea of "making money while you sleep".

<u>Passive income</u>
Dr Dre released one album in the last ten years (in 2015). In 2019, he was named the top earning musician of the decade, earning an estimated US$950 million predominantly in passive income from his 20% stake in the headphone maker Beats. Passive income requires little effort to maintain, whereas active income is earned when you exchange your time for money. The idea behind passive income is to find ways of working that are a little bit smarter. There is a statistic that wealthy people have an average of seven streams of income. Traditionally, passive income came from renting out a property or receiving dividends from investments, both of which require capital investment up-front. Today, passive

earnings come in other formats, most of them mentioned in preceding chapters, but here's a recap of the best:

- Digital courses. There's massive sales growth in digital courses. If you make three sales of a digital course per month from your website, you could net $100+ per month in passive income.
- Affiliate links.
- eBooks. It's possible to create and market 'How To' books in popular niches, building a fan-base of people eager to snap up every new eBook you produce.
- Print-on-demand account or shop. Create three of your own designs for t-shirts or mugs. You could net $6 per item per time and keep building your own branded product.
- Run a blog. Check out the story of Desirae Odjick of www.halfbanked.com
- Create an app.
- Create YouTube videos. Matthew Ross turned his hobby (and source of passive income) into a business by reviewing wearable technology on YouTube. www.rizknows.com

It may take some work to set up passive income streams, but once created they require little effort to maintain. Creating stuff tends to lead to PASSIVE INCOME.

Find passive income ideas on www.oberlo.co.uk. Whichever way you earn, consider checking your tax status with an accountant.

<u>Tips to help you catch the wave</u>

- Expect to have several careers in a lifetime. Be prepared for consultancy style assignments as companies increasingly outsource specialised tasks.

- Studying STEM subjects (science, technology, engineering and maths) will give you a leg–up in the digital economy.

- STEM isn't the whole story of skills for the twenty-first century. While the need for technical expertise remains strong, ensure you develop strong skills in communication, interpretation, design and creative thinking. STEM becomes STEAM with the addition of the letter A to designate the arts (Josh Bersin, Catch the Wave: The 21st Century Career. From Deloitte Review, issue 21). Many young people I've spoken to need reassurance that it's okay to love the arts. In the 2020s, arts subjects are increasingly enmeshed with digital networks, tv shows, games, music and online courses. Skills like photography, design, videography, graphics, animation, content writing and interpersonal and communication skills are as saleable in the internet economy as coding or software development.

The most competent people demonstrate hybrid skills e.g. email marketers and campaign managers need to understand CRM Customer Relationship Management software and marketing automation tools but also need to create content. Great photographers must understand the science of lighting and angles. Brian Cox' outstanding television series "Forces of Nature" would not have come to life without the combination of the creative talent involved in the visual and written storytelling and the scientific expertise of Cox and, BBC Head of Science, Andrew Cohen.

More career ideas

<u>Online Consultant</u>

If you have an online presence with dedicated followers on any platform, if you know how to make a post or video go viral, if you love analysing the data and testing the performance of content (like Sammi Manoff), you could consult to companies who need to develop an online presence and who need help with their online workload. Work in the Blogging, eCommerce, Podcasting, YouTube, Instagram, Twitter, Pinterest, Social Media, TikTok space, selling your expertise in setting up and running a successful account.

<u>Videographer/video producer</u>

Videographers are hugely in demand for the thousands of entrepreneurs selling products and services online who are currently investing huge amounts of money to find good video producers. As people increasingly move into online course provision or selling their products online, they require the help of videographers to sell their wares. Understanding lighting and camera angles will be increasingly marketable.

<u>Copywriter (and content writer)</u>

There are multiple ways you can develop a career as a writer. If you're adept at language and have good writing and grammar skills, consider getting yourself hired to write for a living. Make a start posting articles on Twitter and Facebook. Get paid work by submitting articles to www.medium.com or any of the publications mentioned in Chapter 1. Many businesses will source content creators (and copywriters) on the internet so sign up to www.upwork.com or www.fiverr.com. Publications are crying out for freelancers to submit articles either on a regular basis or periodically. There is an ever-increasing need for copy to populate websites, blogs, Twitter campaigns, long-form Instagram posts and Facebook articles for businesses. Career paths in writing can vary dramatically. Some examples include scriptwriting, becoming a novelist, screenwriting, speech writing and editing. If crafting words is your hobby, there are opportunities to monetise it.

Graphic designer

Many of you are adept at using Canva and other apps to create dynamic images which can be used for businesses and websites to use for advertising. This requires that you put together colours, images and words in a creative way to send the right message to the audience. Depending on who the client is, this can be hugely interesting and great fun. Check out Upwork for jobs.

If you've taken a visual arts course at school and are good at art or have a qualification in art from university, create a portfolio of your best work to show off your artistic skills and get yourself on Upwork (or equivalent). You could also check out online graphic design courses or do a course on how to use Adobe Illustrator. Whatever way you do it, either with a great portfolio or a certification, you know that the more you have to offer, the greater your chances of being hired.

Comedy writer

Many new comedians are building careers on Twitter with 280-character funny insights and jokes. So, if you're clever with words and funny to boot, try giving platform comedy a shot as a pathway to paid work doing what you love.

Instagram shop owner

A friend of mine sells his mini art on Instagram. Instagram is a great place to post original artwork and get a lot of responses and shares. If you have items that Instagram users would like, you can set up a shop by connecting your account to the service Inselly. Once you add the #Inselly tag to your product description, users will find your buyable content. Alternatively, you can post a link in your bio on Instagram. Check out https://neilpatel.com/blog/bootstrap-instagram-selling/. If your art goes viral you can start to sell your products through an online store like Etsy or Shopify.

Social media manager

Increasingly companies are outsourcing their social media presence. Look for social media opportunities on job sites to find openings.

Running YouTube channels

If you have disposable funds, some young entrepreneurs buy and manage YouTube channels for a living. In other words, they might buy a dozen channels in niches where advertisers pay a lot of money and employ graphic designers, commentators, editors, scriptwriters to produce content to continue to populate the channels which they've acquired. This is a lucrative business netting upwards of US$10k (or equivalent) per month depending on the number of channels you own and how much traction you get on those channels.

Facebook expert

Many companies solely use Facebook for their online marketing and PR. If you understand AdWords, SEO, how to analyse your Facebook data and how to build an audience, you will easily find interesting, enjoyable work on Facebook or as an associate of Facebook. Check out the work of Natasha Courtenay-Smith, an accredited Facebook trainer (and CEO of Bolt Digital). www.boltdigital.media

Provider of online courses

If you have a screen and access to the internet, you can provide online courses teaching anything from running webinars to building an Instagram audience to guitar playing. You can teach your course live over Zoom or package your course into a digital product (go to Thinkific.com and search How to create and sell an online course) and sell it from your website.

Online health guru

Many young adults are cashing in on the interest in health food and exercising for health which, just a decade ago, you would have found very difficult to sell. If you love working out and helping others to get fit, this market might work for you. Check out the stratospheric rise of Joe Wicks, who was already building a lucrative career for himself pre-pandemic but has seen a meteoric rise in popularity in 2020. During lockdown, Joe kept adults and children entertained and healthy with his fitness routines and his simple but inspired menus. On the 11th of May 2020, it was reported that Nike and Adidas were allegedly in a £5 million bidding war for an endorsement deal with Joe. You don't have to be an influencer to work this space, but you do need an angle (something that makes you stand out from the crowd). Check out www.thebodycoach.com for inspiration.

Online book reviewer

Check out Jesse George who is famed for reviewing books aimed at young people. She can also be found on YouTube under Jessethereader. Another famous online reviewer is Christine Riccio. Check out her YouTube channel Polandbananasbooks. If you're a bookworm and have a facility with words you might be the British, American or Australian equivalent of Jesse the Reader!

<u>Create a product that fills a gap in the market</u>
Ben Francis did just this when he couldn't find the gym kit he wanted to wear on the high street. He made the kit from scratch with some of his school friends from a room at his parents' home.

<u>Online beauty guru</u>
Do you love makeup? Early in 2017, the New York Times posed the question "Is Huda Kattan the most influential beauty blogger in the world?" They were referring to the young Iraqi-American makeup mogul with over 20 million followers on Instagram. Huda regularly treats her followers to makeup tutorials and insider beauty tips. Of course, her massive online following also helps her to sell makeup in real life. The Huda Beauty Line is sold the world over from Dubai to Hong Kong to London.

<u>Gaming videos</u>
Do you love gaming? Check out Mark Fischbach (aka Markiplier), the Hawaii-born gamer with 17 million subscribers on his gaming videos. He frequently plays for charity events and has been named Forbes's top gaming influencer in the world. In 2016, Fischbach joined Disney's Maker Studios and is one of the most successful career gamers in the world.

<u>Twitch streaming</u>
Twitch is the leading live streaming platform for gamers in which you can watch other people play. If you have 300 to 500 people watching your Twitch channel for most of the stream then you can think about monetising it via donations, brand partnerships and game sales amongst others. Twitch allows viewers to send you donations and tips through integrated services that viewers use for the transaction. Brands approach popular

Twitch streamers to get their products in front of large audiences and pay you for this. If you're a streamer you might include a brand in a sponsored stream title, on a tile on your channel page or include a brand placement on the video stream itself.

Kindle self-publishing

You could self-publish on Amazon using the Kindle self-publishing platform and become a full-time novelist. Amazon takes care of technical details. You provide the completed document, add a cover image and description and Amazon does the rest. The fortunes of James Redfield "The Celestine Prophecy" and EL James' the "50 Shades" Series were built on the Kindle self-publishing platform.

Teaching online

If you have the relevant qualifications this can be lucrative. Check out these sites www.vipkid.com and www.mytutor.co.uk or www.supertutoring.co.uk. Tutoring online can be a full-time or part-time job, you work from home and it's flexible.

Non-profit work

Working in non-profit organisations can be very rewarding (especially if you're passionate about helping people and have been involved in voluntary work at school or as a young adult). Making a difference in the lives of fellow humans or animals has high fulfilment value and also gives you invaluable life experience. There are many roles and many different areas that you can work in within this sector: (check out www.charityjob.co.uk or similar where you live)

- Arts and culture
- Health

- Education
- Animals
- Environmental
- Non-government organisations

Training and Resources
<u>Online courses</u>
You now understand that you have to continuously learn, upskill and reskill but I'm sure you're wondering how to make that happen. Over the past decade, online training has exploded with "edtech" companies receiving millions of dollars of investment from investors. There are technical education sites such as General Assembly, Skillsoft and Pluralsight, online course providers such as Udacity and Coursera, Hubspot Academy, LinkedIn Learning, knowledge-sharing sites such as Udemy and free eLearning on YouTube, Pinterest and openlearn.com. The need to continuously reskill is made so much easier by the presence of low-cost courses, lessons and expert education online. You can learn a new skill from the comfort of your living room. Or from the comfort of your office desk if you happen to work for an innovative company like Visa or IBM where internal MOOCs enable you to shop within your own company for any training that you need. Check out the website <u>www.openlearn.com</u>, a free resource with hundreds of courses for you to try out.

A word of caution about online gurus. In this space, there are lots of good salespeople hyping it up and making it sound super easy to build a business and have huge success online. It's because they sell courses for a living. Many young people have reservations about online courses and course claims. The challenge in choosing an online course provider is to distinguish between the great teachers (often with many years of experience in the business, who want to pay it forward with free content as well as paid-for courses) and the salespeople with smooth pitches. It's important to do due diligence before paying for any course. Perhaps the best way for now whilst you're starting out is to follow people who constantly give you valuable, free content whether you buy from them or not. When finances allow, buy a paid-for course from them. An insider tip is to check that the person you buy from is themselves the course provider. Also check that you'll have access to them for the duration of the course. Ask in online communities if anyone has worked with them before. Ask your peers.

The good news is there is a lot of free education to consume online shared by people who want to help. The best of the online experts provide unbelievable value, whether in the freebies they readily share or in their paid courses.

<u>Apprenticeships</u>
Apprenticeships can very quickly fast-track your career and have been patently underestimated as a tool to

kickstart careers. Not any longer! Fortunately, there are some amazing people and organisations working in this space. In the UK, check out NGTU at www.notgoingtouni.co.uk for information about all kinds of apprenticeships from degree apprenticeships (yes, they exist) to higher apprenticeships and more. Multiverse is an organisation that operates in the UK and internationally. It offers an alternative to university, measuring your potential beyond academics and work experience (useful if you're kickstarting your career) and provides world-class, job-focused training. Check them out here www.multiverse.io. Multiverse (in its previous incarnation as White Hat) has already fast-tracked hundreds of young people into building fulfilling and lucrative careers. If you're undecided about going to university but not quite ready to dive into employment or entrepreneurship, apprenticeships offer you experience, mentors, training, a salary and an amazing community of future friends. Make sure to download the Fledglink app (detailed in full below) which will keep you updated with live information about apprenticeships, job opportunities and life after education!

Networking
Networking is crucial in managing your career whether you work for yourself, a multi-national or a small startup. LinkedIn is caters to professionals with extensive industry experience (do sign up to LinkedIn anyway), but when kickstarting your career you need networks of people of a similar age with similar ambitions and skills and you need links to employers. Below are some brilliant apps which you should sign up to:

Fledglink
Fledglink was established by Ellie Yell, a business psychologist, to connect students and young people with

exciting employment opportunities, helpful resources, apprenticeship guides, personality questionnaires, interview guides and much more. **Fledglink is a professional, educational network for sixteen to twenty-four-year-olds connecting young people to job opportunities, providing them with a chance to network with other ambitious young adults, smoothing entry into employment by helping them to develop their abilities, increase self-awareness and confidence and unlock inner strengths.** Sign up to Fledglink at www.fledglink.com and start networking today. Navigate to the job board to find entry-level and school-leaver jobs. You can find internships and apprenticeships on Fledglink too. Complete your dashboard in the "My CV" section and you'll be smart-matched to relevant opportunities. It's worth investigating degree apprenticeships if you want a degree without incurring student debt. As an example, it's now possible for a would-be lawyer to take an apprenticeship route all the way from leaving school to gaining a qualification as a solicitor. Traditionally the only way to become a solicitor would be through the university route.

www.daisie.com

Daisie is a talent discovery app and website for the arts which was created by Maisie Williams of "Game of

Thrones" fame. It's a creative network – like Fledglink but for the arts.

www.the-dots.com
The-dots has been described as a network for professional people who don't wear suits to work! Sign up to the-dots to get advice, find collaborators, network with other university graduates, land your dream job in social media marketing or website design or find jobs at the BBC or Channel 4.

Old-fashioned networking
Don't forget about the old-school things that still work. Attend conferences, film screenings, job fairs, VidCon for YouTubers, Social Media Week, Digital Summit, BeautyCon. Go to www.eventbrite.com and check out social media conferences or talent recruitment events where you live.

Next steps if this is for you
Big Tech, multinational organisations, consultancy firms
If you've not been drawn to a career as an entrepreneur, influencer or social media manager, working for corporates may feel like the right move for you now. If you're not ready to found your own business yet, having the right employer can be a ticket to great things. You might be interested in getting a full-time job, an internship, an apprenticeship or a graduate role working for companies like IBM, Disney, Lego, Microsoft, Visa, Alphabet, McKinsey, Apple (Apple employees in the UK went through lockdown on full pay with lots of perks). Alternatively, you might approach startups for interesting work and sell your services consulting to an entrepreneur or an influencer. All of these options guarantee you opportunities for continuous learning, great individual mobility, access to internal massive open online courses

(MOOCs) so you can get any training you need on the job. The big companies will also offer you free access to online courses by providers such as Coursera, edX, Udacity, Novoed, and Udemy so you can learn from the comfort of your office.

Take care to match yourself to environments that fit you best. If you value security and certainty (as much as that's possible) over risk and the possibility of failure, then you might better enjoy putting your ambitions and talents to use working within a multinational than setting up on your own. The trade-off of working for someone else is it may not bring you the spoils (or satisfaction) of making your own business work for you but there are undoubted benefits and entrepreneurship may beckon later.

Don't be shy to apply for jobs without a degree. For certain roles, your skillset is equally valuable to employers. In a recent interview with Steve Brooks in Enterprise Times Magazine, Ben Towers commented that he's drawn to candidates who have grown up on social media and know intuitively how to use it (who know how to tweet or do an Instagram post and get people to like it). He made the point that it's easier to take on the responsibility of teaching someone the commercial side than to teach someone social networking. https://www.enterprisetimes.co.uk/2017/03/22/ben-towers-ceo-and-founder-towers-design/

No drastic action is required from you to bridge the gap between education and work. Think about what you're good at. **TAKE ONE SMALL STEP TOWARDS MASTERING ONE AREA.** Once you know everything about it, use that expertise to solve a problem for someone. This is the route to finding a job. Network on Fledglink, research small companies to spot gaps in which to insert yourself and your skills. Is their website any good? Do they even have a website? If not, offer to build one. Is their social media any good? Offer to do two posts per day on all their social media channels for US$50 (£40) per week, or more if you have a proven track record for driving traffic to a site and increasing sales. Check out marketing emails of brands you love. Are their emails good? How could they be better? Offer to write their emails for them for a fee. How about the marketing strategy of that fancy local café you love? Is it effective? Offer to do it for them for a fee.

CHAPTER 11
THE GIG ECONOMY

HOW, HAVING STUDIED ILLUSTRATION AT UNIVERSITY, DELPHINE JONES FOUND A WAY TO JUGGLE A JOB AS A FREELANCER WITH A PART-TIME JOB SHE LOVES.

Delphine, who is from the UK, worked in arts marketing for five years when she finished her degree, towards the end of which she cut down her hours to take a nine-month job producing an arts festival. Today she works two jobs; as a theatre programmer for The Lyric Theatre in Bridport one day a week, and as a freelance illustrator and graphic designer the rest of her working week. Delphine enjoys the variety of work and how the theatre job contrasts with her freelancing role, in giving her the opportunity to work as part of a team. To date, the work has been fairly constant. Delphine has been able to identify peaks and troughs in demand at certain times, which has made her more relaxed about not having a regular monthly income. She lives in a small market town and says that most of the people she knows have multiple jobs and are largely self-employed. Like Alice, Delphine features in the book because, as a young businesswoman, she has found a way to work the digital economy to her advantage, managing a business and a style of working and earning which fits the lifestyle she wants right now. Check Delphine out at www.delphinejones.com

The gig economy is characterised by working multiple jobs at the same time. Compare that with the idea of multiple careers, characterised by working a job for 5 years before switching to another job. A gig is essentially a short-term exchange of labour for immediate payment. You do pieces of work for one or a variety of contractors and essentially you are classified in the same way as a freelancer. There are different ways of working the gig economy according to your lifestyle and goals. Like Delphine, you can work multiple gigs as a freelancer and combine that with a regular part-time job, or gig on the side combining that with a full-time job or alternatively, do multiple gigs to the equivalent of full-time hours. If you advertise yourself as a freelancer on an online platform like Fiverr, you're notified when you get an order, use the platform to discuss the requirement with the client and get paid on order completion. Making money online in any format, requires entrepreneurial skills, focus and discipline, however the upside of working in the gig economy is that you don't have to invest two years of your time before earning. Working a gig is different from a traditional way of earning but it's a trade-off — gigs give you flexibility and control over your time, but no guaranteed income. Many people do gigs alongside a full-time or part-time job (as Delphine does) or invest time in uncovering passive income streams to bolster earn ls to work the gproof your working life, it's worth considering both:

- Having multiple careers (a series of careers in response to market demands or a switch to a long-held passion as Alice beautifully demonstrated), and
- Working gigs (either jobs on-the-side or setting yourself up as a freelancer).

It's easy to think of the gig economy as a nice little way to earn extra money but it's actually significantly disrupting the world of work. Easy access to tools that help you run a freelance business and work-for-hire platforms that connect you with available jobs are changing work habits in a major way. Gigs are increasingly looking like the future of work, which sounds scarier than it is. We're doing the work we always do but delivering it differently. You'll master skills to work the gig economy such as:

- Becoming literate in digital technology
- Developing entrepreneurial skills to see and seize opportunities in the market
- Learning the skills necessary to become self-starting and to match yourself to relevant jobs and market yourself to get them.

Companies like ebay, Airbnb, Etsy and Uber have created opportunities for thousands of people to work side gigs. It's a way to have a stream of income to support cashflow. Young people are reporting earning up to eight thousand pounds in the year from gigs such as buying and selling on eBay, selling social media services or proofreading essays on Fiverr (take the time to get your Fiverr profile description right e.g. I'm a First-Class Honours English Graduate or an A★ English student). The pay isn't great but earning extra money from the comfort of your home is an attractive proposition. Whether you've never had a job, had your hours cut from a weekend job, are interested in testing out multiple different jobs as career research, want money to help pay your fees or simply want to keep your options open, there is a gig out there for you. The beauty of a gig is that you can earn money whilst you wait to see how your job interview went or whilst you write articles for Medium.com. If you can make more money doing a gig than working a nine-to-five job for someone, consider turning it into your main job with all the freedom that working your own hours entails. Keep your options open and try as many side gigs as you can. You can get paid minimum wage to watch YouTube videos, design logos or teach maths. Some gigs are scalable and could be notched up to create a steady source of income.

The go-to expert for young people in the gig market is Sarah Chrisp. Sarah is best known for her hugely popular YouTube Channel Wholesale Ted, in which she shares videos about how to build an online business. She knows every side-gig trick in the business. She makes money online in several ways including sales of products from several of her own online Shopify stores. Check out Sarah's videos on YouTube. Gigs are the perfect way to test out a new skill or try out different jobs with no commitment. Offline gigs (like driving for Uber, house sitting or dog walking) tend to pay better to start with, but online gigs come with the benefit of working from home which cuts down your costs and can blow up into something very successful over time. It's worth making a detailed business plan and consulting an accountant if this business model appeals to you.

Gigs

Teach English

If you're in the UK sign up to Education First at www.ef.com. They like to book lessons in blocks of four to eight weeks which is useful if you want to plan your income over some time. You need a basic Degree (not necessarily in English) and a TEFL qualification (Teach English as a Foreign Language) or equivalent. You can do an online TEFL course for as little as £19 (84% discount) through www.boostmybudget.com. You earn from £8.50-£12.50 per twenty-five-minute class. In the United States, you can earn US$17-$22 per hour to teach English to kids in China at www.vipkid.com (several of the big-name companies only recruit within the US). A big advantage of both Education First and VipKid is that they have their own curriculum for you to follow, so you don't have to plan your own classes each week. Most people do two twenty-five-minute classes per hour. Also check out iTalki, a platform where freelance tutors can find students. On iTalki you can find work as a professional teacher or as a community tutor. As a community tutor, you can teach English (if you are a native English speaker) without a degree or a TEFL certification so this is great if you're just starting out.

Note: If your student doesn't show, you get paid to do your own thing (surf the net, catch up with your friends!) although you have to stay on the call.

<u>Social media consultant</u>
If you're a user on social media platforms and already have over 5,000 subscribers, you can earn money building a social media platform for someone else (either as a career or as a gig). As a consumer, you know how social media works, what captivates your attention, how a person or company gets you to follow them or click on their page and you have built your own following, so why not reverse engineer it and offer to help someone else do that for a fee (either on a retainer basis or commission basis). Find a business whose social media is not very good and send them a video outlining what you think they should do to make it better. Make suggestions: you could fix this to get more traction, try this ad, post this type of social media, etc. **You can do this for companies before you have any formal marketing training, if you can show stats for your own account.** Put a description of what you're offering on Fiverr. If you've earned money on Fiverr, from the selling menu, click earnings. You will have options to withdraw your earnings via PayPal or bank transfer.

Freelancing

If you have a skillset, why not make money from it by being a freelancer? Use platforms like Fiverr or Upwork. This will give you great business experience. If you're good at art, you can do logos or draw a portrait of someone or do caricatures. You can do web development, work as a VA, write SEO articles, create websites, illustrate, make thumbnails for videos, transcribe videos, create graphics or write content. Fiverr and Upwork take a commission – on the main platforms your reviews go up as you go, so you'll get repeat business. If you get enough work, why not set up on your own with your own website and your own list of clients? For many young people their full-time freelancing business started out as gig work.

The best part of freelancing is you manage your own time. The trade-off is that you don't have guaranteed income but with online business booming during the pandemic there is no shortage of gigs.

Temping

Temping is an amazing route to finding a job you may not have considered, without making any formal commitment to the company. Moving between companies, changing roles and sectors as you go, gives you extensive first-hand experience and the opportunity to discover work environments and conditions that you might prefer. Do temp work whilst you research work options and tutor in the evenings. Temping roles are increasingly remote but, in some cases, you may have to travel to work and be physically present. Temping is not officially a gig as you earn regular income from one employer, but it provides some of the same advantages as gig work.

Internet researcher

You can make money by finding information for companies or individuals who don't have time to spend doing the research themselves. Typically, you'll find research jobs using a platform like Upwork (you can find literally up to five thousand research jobs posted on there, such as gathering background material for writers and journalists or summarising book plots) and get paid on delivery. On Upwork if you've earned money, navigate to Payment Options and select PayPal (or equivalent) from amongst the options.

Write articles for Medium

If your article gets traction you get paid. People tend to write for Medium when they're starting out as the work is not well paid, but it makes you a published writer. I've signed up to this platform and read articles on it daily. Log in to enjoy the mental stimulation. If you're a writer, good with catchy titles and subtitles and can churn out a few articles per week, join Medium's Partner Programme to earn money. Check out Tim Denning for training on how to make money from writing for Medium (www.timdenning.com).

Logo designer

Most of you are familiar with the free and paid tech to create logo designs. Some startups who don't have time or money to invest in a top-quality designer will pay small sums to people on Fiverr or Upwork to design logos for them. You would need to pay close attention to what the client wants, provide them with drafts and then deliver the finished product once they choose the logo they want. Check out logo providers on Fiverr to find out the going rates and what they offer. If you're good at logos, copy that format and get your profile on there.

<u>Sell products on Printify or CaféPress</u>
Printify (one of the best printers to use if you're in the UK) is a print-on-demand platform that makes it easy to work with printers in various countries to fulfil and send your products to your customers. With Printify (unlike CaféPress) you have to set up shop on a selling platform like Etsy and integrate it with your Printify account (it's free to set up an account and the integration process is easy). You design the t-shirt or mug on Printify and upload it to your shop. When a customer buys your product on Etsy, an order is automatically sent to Printify and they print and dispatch the item to the customer. (Choose a UK-based printer if your customers are in the UK). You pay the printers a fee for printing, labour and postage and keep the rest.

CaféPress is a free online merchandising shop. Like eBay, CaféPress is a destination website selling everything from mugs to t-shirts and hoodies (shipping is from the USA and shows US$ currency). As it's a destination website you don't have to advertise your product and you don't have to have a physical product. Once you open a free CaféPress account, simply go to the designs page and do a design. If you're not great at design, you can do simple text (just be careful of copyright infringement). Once you design something it's yours, so you can upload your

design to CaféPress and also to other websites. You

own the rights to your design. Once you make a design for a t-shirt or a mug or hoodie or all three, CaféPress will create a product listing for you and once someone clicks the buy button, they will produce it, package it and ship it to the buyer. The way you get paid is the website hosting your t-shirt (in this instance CaféPress) receives the money from the client, takes their fee and pays the difference to you.

This is a good way for young people to get into business because you don't need an inventory of hoodies, t-shirts or mugs and nor do you need a t-shirt printer or a website. Many teens are making huge money selling cute face masks right now. You can make a few hundred pounds a month once you hit on the right product or the right slogan.

Print-on-demand is your friend. Your design is printed on inventory you don't own, once customers place an order. You never have to have the physical t-shirt yourself.

Some teens are not put off by having to source and print the t-shirt themselves. During lockdown Sidney, seventeen, and Ossie O'Neill, fifteen, from Brighton in the United Kingdom bought forty plain t-shirts, borrowed a heat press and embossed three designs onto the t-shirts which they'd created using Adobe Photoshop. They advertised on Facebook and Instagram and set up a store on Shopify (£30 per month, free for the first month) and their t-shirts sold out within the month (no Shopify costs). From an original investment of £100, the brothers made a profit of £500. (https://www.theguardian.com/money/2020/oct/17/teen-entrepreneurs-defying-covid-slump)

Transcribe videos and write captions

You don't need any qualifications to sign up to transcribe video files and make money. Sign up to Transcriptdivas.co.uk or Mcgowantranscription.co.uk if you're UK-based, or Rev.com or Gotranscript.com to transcribe videos and write captions. There are tutorials you can watch online to teach you how to be a transcriber. A reputable transcriber can earn up to £1200 per month in the UK and approximately US$1,000 per month in the US. Getting paid to listen to podcasts and videos or write captions is big business and a way to earn consistently. Rev closes its applications from time to time but check back until they re-open. The best gigs are found during the week so check the site then.

User testing

Companies will pay you to test out their website (or apps) to see how you respond to it. Does the landing page make sense? Do you know where to click to find products or to get to the checkout? Can you find the product you're searching for quickly and easily? You might be required to give feedback on games, apps, customer services or complaints. Sign up to www.usertesting.com to give feedback and help designers know if a user can navigate around a site well and understand the functionality. You can earn up to 30 dollars an hour for this which is paid into a PayPal account. Simply register, provide your PayPal details and you will receive your payment seven days after completing a website test or an app test (this allows usertesting.com an opportunity to check the quality of the recordings). It's best to sign up for gigs that pay you in your currency. Otherwise, check out TransferWise. It's not a bank but is authorised by the Financial Conduct Authority (FCA) in the UK, like high-street banks are. They give a fair market exchange rate, but you may still be charged a fee by your bank.

Home-based call centre agent
This is good if you have somewhere quiet to work in your house and a laptop with a good internet provider. You set your own hours and get paid for hours worked. www.reed.co.uk or www.glassdoor.com.

Do online surveys
These are the easiest way to make small amounts of money. In the USA www.SurveySavvy.com comes recommended for sending you the most surveys although each one is in the range of US$1–5. On Reddit people report earning up to US$80 per month. In the UK try www.Swagbucks.com or www.OpinionOutpost.co.uk to earn up to £60 per month. You'll need a lot of spare time to earn this amount of money from surveys.

Sell stuff on Depop or ebay
There are lots of niche apps if you want to sell unused items or little-worn clothes. You could also sell products

you create. My daughter's friend sells hand-crafted items on Etsy.com that she designs herself.

Online or telephone focus groups

Make money from home by offering your opinion on something online or you may receive a product to use and report back on what you thought of the product. When you register with a research organisation specify whether you prefer to work in in-person groups or online, by text or telephone.

Write articles

Freelance writing, despite being active work, is a good way to earn an income online. If you have 'the superpower' why not offer to write for larger websites? Or log onto www.textbroker.com or www.textbroker.co.uk and sign up for different writing gigs. You get paid based on the number of words you write. You're assigned a level. Most people get a 4★ rating immediately, but a team of people at Textbroker constantly rate your articles so your rating (and consequently your pay) can increase. If you can write 1000 words an hour, you earn US$40/£30 (more if you have a 5★ rating) via your PayPal account. Textbroker is one of the most popular sites and you don't need a professional background in writing to offer your services on here. You could check out www.writeraccess.com if you're a graduate (they sell themselves as proven, professional writers). If you have the superpower it makes no difference whether you have a degree or not. Sign up for all the platforms if you want to write for a living. Another option is to sign up to www.fiverr.com as a content writer. Where possible sign up for gigs that pay you in your currency. Otherwise, check out TransferWise which was mentioned previously.

<u>Sell your photos</u>
If you're good at photography, people will pay you good money to use your photos. Shutterstock is a global marketplace for artists and creators to sell royalty-free images, footage and illustrations. Check them out at <u>www.submit.shutterstock.com</u>. Check out the deal too at Flickr which is a popular place to view photos. You can license your photos under Creative Commons which will expose your photos to a wider audience although it won't net you money. <u>www.flicker.com/creativecommons/</u>. It's good for building authority.

<u>Become an online tutor as a graduate</u>
Sign up to <u>www.skooli.com</u> or sign up through www.reed.co.uk, www.tutorful.co.uk or <u>www.tutor.com</u> for teaching gigs for people with a university degree. You set up a profile and when students send out a request you hop into the market to get a gig. These sites tend to offer immediate work as there are so many tutoring requests. Tutor pays less than Skooli and Tutorful but you can expect to earn £20–30 and approximately US$25 an hour working from the comfort of your home.

<u>Shout-outs</u>
If you have a strong presence on Instagram, you can **get paid for a 24-hour shout-out to your followers.** US$250 (c.£200) for between 100k–500k followers, US$1000 (£750) for upwards of 500k followers. If your tribe is made up of committed followers, some businesses will pay you even if you have only1000 followers, usually in the region of US$35 (£26) per shout-out. If you market using story promo, a shout-out plus pictures videos, you could end up earning up to US$135 in 24 hours. Your followers may buy, subscribe to or simply follow the other account. If you have a huge, committed audience in the same field as another user,

they might pay you a significant amount of money for a shout-out.

Create YouTube videos

YouTube can make you lots of money as long as people want to see your content. You need to start now to build your subscribers, you will need 1000 subscriptions as a starting point. **Teens are making money on popular YouTube channels through affiliate commissions and Google AdSense** (sign up, enter the URL of the site you want to show ads on. You receive a code to copy and paste onto your website and Google pays you any time someone clicks on your ads). For affiliate commissions www.siteground.com is one of the highest payers. Sign up and you'll get a URL to pop on your YouTube account. If you then make say a video tutorial, you insert the affiliate link in the video description and when someone clicks on it, you get a commission that is paid directly to your bank account.

Display ads

These are similar to Google AdSense but the reader doesn't have to click on the ad for you to make money. You receive money based on the number of times your ads are viewed. Open your Google ad account and click "display campaigns" then ads.

Buy and sell websites

People buy and sell websites for any number of reasons. GoDaddy regularly advertise websites that are for sale. Also check out Flippa.com. Check out what to look for here: https://www.hostgator.com/blog/how-to-sell-a-website/

Create a course

The online education industry is growing and is predicted to be a 300-billion-dollar industry by 2025! If you set up an account on Teachable it's free. Click "Try our Free Plan" then record enough clips to have your own video course for free. And place your affiliate link in the video description with a link to where people can buy the video course you've made via Teachable. You can get paid by Stripe or straight into your bank account. You can also sell courses on Coursera or Udemy. A digital product such as a PDF, an eBook, a video series or course, once created, can earn you money whilst you sleep.

The way we earn money has changed. Increasingly, you're not compensated for time spent sitting at a desk but for a piece of professionally produced work that can be sent from Katmandu (internet connection permitting) to the person who contracted you for the job. (Post-pandemic remote working is becoming a standard even in more traditional work roles.) Whether you're marketing, writing content, dropshipping products or analysing or solving problems you can accomplish your objective from your laptop.

Next steps if this is for you

Sit down and make a list of jobs you could do now and jobs you would like to do with a little bit of training. Approach people locally who might offer you initial pieces of work to get the ball rolling. Sign up to a work-for-hire platform. Write your profile description for Fiverr. Keep it short. Clearly state what you're offering and what you need from the client in order to get the job done. Check out this article: https://deadlycontent.com/how-to-write-a-gig-description-for-fiverr-that-demands-attention.

Choose a job you might like to do next and sign up for the relevant training.

CHAPTER 12
CONCLUSION

HOW RISHAB JAIN, AT THIRTEEN, DEVELOPED A SOFTWARE TOOL TO HELP DOCTORS ZERO IN ON THE PANCREAS MORE ACCURATELY, IMPROVING PANCREATIC CANCER TREATMENTS.

As Gen Zs, you can change the world. I don't mean in a figurative or imaginary way. From Rishab Jain harnessing AI to improve radiotherapy for cancer patients, to Marley Dias and her successful mission to collect and distribute1000 books featuring black female protagonists to school children, to Greta Thunberg's action on climate change, all of these young people are motivated by a strong sense of moral duty. In 2018, Rishab was named America's Top Young Scientist (3M Young Scientist Challenge 2018). This gifted young man went on to use the money he won to create a non-profit organisation to promote STEM learning for disadvantaged children. Check Rishab out here: www.samyakscience.org.

Ben Towers is on a mission to connect his generation and tackle mental health issues. He co-founded Tahora in a bid to re-imagine mental health and wellbeing in the workplace. Alana Spencer works with The Tenner Challenge, a national competition run by Young Enterprise UK, which aims to develop key skills in young people aged 11–18 including creativity, resilience and problem solving, using real money to take calculated risks in business. Ben Francis, through his company Gymshark, is a generous supporter of various NHS charities. Every one of the people featured in this book, earning everything from prize winnings to moderate to high incomes, have a strong sense of duty about contributing to society. You're a "saving the next generation" generation! You're focused on respecting the environment, protective of others' rights, interested in politics and defining future policies and conscientious about sharing information.

If thinking about your career keeps you awake at night, if the path from study to work seems unclear and leaves you feeling scared and not knowing where to turn, I hope that this book and the ideas and actions of young people like yourself, will help you to take that first, small step. Whether you want to be an entrepreneur, a website designer, a Google employee, an inventor or a doctor via university, an apprenticeship, an online course or a deep dive into the unknown, what is important is that you see a way forward in your journey and challenge your own assumptions about earning and working. In the story of David and Goliath, David dictated the terms of the battle with the giant. No head-to-head combat in which losing was guaranteed. He left the armour behind and killed the giant from a distance, with a slingshot to the head. Be street smart and tackle the digital giant creatively, on your terms.

There is a common misconception that you need to be "special" or a "genius" to be successful. Apple Crider believes that **it's not about being special; most people have something special. The difference lies in "focus and discipline".** That sounds simple but finding and keeping your buyers, your followers, or your eventual employers takes perseverance and effort. Researching products, anticipating what your buyers want vs what they need, living with the uncertainty of knowing whether you read the market right, writing your blog, creating endless posts, videoing, photographing, more research, re-imagining, regrouping, researching jobs, researching employers, making applications and finding contacts, all require focus and discipline. **The young people you see earning well and living a seemingly carefree life have been proactively and consistently chasing their dreams for some time.**

Be honest with yourself. Don't pretend you should be further along than you are if you simply haven't done the work! In the book *The Marshmallow Test*, Walter Mischel talks about the habit of putting business before pleasure. It boils down to being clear about your goals and choosing to forego trips to the pub or the beach in favour of getting things done. Whatever you choose to do, put in the hard work and you will get the reward later. Don't be put off or get distracted from your end goal by the uncomfortable feeling of not knowing stuff, of being out of your depth, of not reaching your goal fast enough. This part of the journey is not supposed to feel comfortable! Comfortable comes later when all the hard work pays off. In the interview in The Guardian, (see page 51), Fleur de Force commented, with great insight, that the work "takes over your life. It is all-consuming; you have to throw yourself into it. That's part of being successful". **Focus and discipline are more common markers of success than having some "special" quality.**

Before we leave the subject of being "special" it's worth pointing out that there are geniuses (genii!) in many disciplines. Technically an IQ of 140 or higher is genius-level intelligence. I'm not going to attribute genius status to people in this book who might not want such a title or approve of the use of such terminology, but I will make an important point: **being a genius isn't the only part of the success puzzle. THERE ARE PLENTY OF GENIUSES SITTING AROUND WATCHING TV.** You have to think of something to use your brain for. It's still about the drive and determination to do something and the focus and discipline to action it rather than how much of a genius you are. Don't get distracted from your goals by thinking you have to be more special than you are or be born a genius.

Ways to Kickstart Your Journey
<u>Ask yourself tough questions about work</u>

Are you risk averse and have high anxiety levels around uncertainty? You may find entrepreneurship challenging. Are you bored by the mundane and constantly seeking new, exciting prospects? Setting up a business may get your creative juices flowing in a way that sitting at a desk never could. If job security is paramount for you, what other criteria are important within that scope? Do you like working alone or with people? Do you prefer to be in an office with friends and colleagues and a ready-made social life on tap or working from home? Find creative solutions. Could you do three days in an office and two days at home? Or line up steady work as a freelancer and use shared workspace so you can see other people at the same time? How much do you want to earn and what are you willing to give up in the short-term to achieve that? Do you want to be extremely wealthy or to earn just enough not to worry about finances? Which jobs can provide you with the earning power you want?

<u>Ask yourself tough questions about study</u>
Should you wish to pursue the traditional university route, consider which university, its reputation and its relationship with employers. What percentages of graduates get jobs upon graduation? Choose a university that has a track record of preparing graduates to enter the workforce. What advantage does a particular degree course offer you? How much will it cost? Will you have a profession afterwards (as a lawyer or an engineer) or are you gaining transferable skills e.g. graduating in classics to go into journalism (and eventually politics which was Boris Johnson's journey)? If so, how do you plan to make money with those transferable skills? If you are academic and love learning, university will bring you joy, but keep a firm eye on how people are earning a living and how you intend to make money in the 2020s economy.

<u>Be creative about finding your ideal job</u>
Dream up innovative ways to adapt to the job market. Simplify what you're good at to as few moving parts as possible. Choose an area in which you either have skills or lots of passion. Follow a few people whom you value and focus on your output. Then get creative. Have you considered the kind of support staff that online stars like Holly H and Joe Wicks will be seeking to employ to help them to grow their businesses? From web designers to social media marketers, from videographers to copywriters, the jobs are out there.

If you want to gain experience working for someone else as you start out, target the person whose work you love and see if you can support them in their career journey. **Show interest in what they do. Why would they want you to work for them if you haven't watched their videos, researched their companies or noticed something in their content that, with a little tweaking, could be better or garner more traffic.** Be willing to do just that little bit extra to help them in their day-to-day life. In "The Devil Wears Prada", Andy, an aspiring journalist takes a job working for the editor of a fashion magazine. She works hard, meeting endless demands and the gruelling schedule of the editor, but eventually the hard work pays off when the devilish editor gives her a glowing reference for her dream job working for a prestigious newspaper.

<u>Match yourself to jobs</u>

Do the research and try to match yourself to the types of jobs out there. What are you passionate about? If you love it, you'll never make the distinction between work and life. Writing, drawing, shooting videos, data science, meeting people, building websites, selling things. Research job boards on Fledglink, Daisie and The-Dots. More traditional boards include <u>www.indeed.com</u>, <u>www.linkedin.com</u>, <u>www.glassdoor.com</u>, <u>www.reed.com</u>, <u>www.simplyhired.com</u>. In the UK <u>www.workinstartups.com</u> is a useful tool. Facebook jobs will show you opportunities in your area and you can apply from your profile (or directly to the organisation if your profile is not work-proofed!). Pinterest is a search engine like Google, as well as a huge learning resource, so type the job you'd like to do into the browser and see what information pops up. You'll find that people have pinned valuable information on there about all sorts of subjects. **Don't be put off if most of the jobs on job boards require experience. If you feel up to the job, apply anyway. Use your online presence to showcase your abilities.**

<u>Learn new skills</u>

If you want to be successful you will need to develop skills that are not currently taught at school, so you have to improvise. Observe what's happening around you. Shifts in consumer behaviour during recent months from arranging meetings on Team to teaching classes on Zoom, from a stratospheric rise in online sales to the rise of the lockdown celebrity (think of Joe Wicks), all of this is the new normal, not least because it's proved convenient. Can you slot your skills into this new market? What do you need to learn to adapt to it?

Check out www.openlearn.com for free courses. Check out courses on Coursera or Udemy (see suggestions in Chapter 10). Network for all your worth. Ask for help, connect to people on Fledglink, Daisie and The-Dots to talk to people in the same position as yourself. Find articles online, read books, email questions to me at fiona@cosmikos.com and check out articles on www.cosmikos.com. Do gigs from your laptop to make money whilst you're learning. Some gigs will turn out to be a simple way to make extra cash and some gigs may turn out to be scalable and become a full-time job.

Have a flexible career plan – Adapt it to fit the environment
There are plenty of jobs outside of traditional roles. The reality is that you may not discover what you love doing before the age of forty! To seize opportunities, you have to see opportunities. You should always be on the lookout for new ideas and know where government think-tanks and thought-leaders in the world of online business are focusing their attention. Keep up to date with the ideas of Jeff Walker, Marie Forleo, Steven Essa, Gary Vaynerchuk, Kimra Luna. Follow their advice.

It's okay not to have a career plan
You don't have to be bursting with business ideas or do anything drastic now. Everyone's different. You may not be ready to make a major career decision. It's okay not to know (be proud of yourself for getting to this point, for finishing formal study and looking to the future, for reading this book). Just as the entrepreneurs and influencers featured in this

book are at different stages, school-leavers and graduates are at different stages too. Some are on the starting blocks all set to work or study or set up in business. Some are slow burners and need to try out different jobs to figure themselves out. Many hugely successful people became entrepreneurs later in life. You have options. Just don't sit still. Choose to learn one thing to move the needle a little bit.

In meantime...

Learn how to use your computer to make some cash. Learn everything you can about dropshipping. Try out a few different gigs. You can make a living whether you go to university or not, you can earn money whilst you study or do gigs whilst you work. You can become a lawyer and at the same time create a life-changing app, you can backpack and trade in eCommerce, you can attend lectures and sell your paintings via your online business. You can work gigs from home, scheduling your own hours whilst you figure out what you want. You can network on Fledglink. You can manage a fledgling business or await a much sought-after job offer whilst you do a free course. You can have a passive source of income and do a few weekly gigs to make up multiple income streams. Choose what's right for you. With a laptop, a WiFi connection, and a little bit of self-belief*, anything is possible.

*Self-belief is the belief that you can complete tasks and achieve your goals. Focus on one goal e.g. blogging. Make a list of what you need to learn and do and start to become a blogger. You're part-way there. Get it going one step at a time. Check out www.cosmikos.com for tips on daily habits for success and how to get the list done.

Navigate your route

Consider the following when navigating and planning your route:

- Find what you like doing best. Find someone to pay you for doing it.

- Don't be embarrassed about changing your mind, your career, or your profession. The world is shifting beneath us and pivoting is smart. Many of the most successful people have changed direction repeatedly.

- If you have an idea for a business, test it, or talk to someone you trust about your idea, research the market, get help to draw up a business plan, research ways of raising funds and educate yourself in the niche. Choose a field of opportunity that is growing not declining.

- Ask for advice but don't let family, teachers or friends persuade you to study or work at something that you know in your gut is not right for you.

- Even if you intend to become a lawyer, an engineer or a scientist, try to leave time for entrepreneurial pursuits within your career. You're living in the project economy where job switching is commonplace. Be ready to pivot to become an author, tv host or artist later on.

You're not in the hope market

There is little point in sitting around hoping for a job or buyers or followers to fall into your lap. If you're a ship's captain, you don't cross your fingers and hope you'll arrive at your destination; you navigate the best route by learning the currents and planning your trip. Choose something to do, one thing, that you can become the best at. It will feel uncomfortable. **It's not supposed to feel good. What feels good is when you get to the other side and realise you've started a blog or have sold**

your first product. Thanks to the internet there is every chance of actioning your plan. Don't stay on the sidelines watching whilst others make progress. You don't want to be in the same place next year thinking *I should have started twelve months ago.* Focus on one opportunity. It won't be perfect the first few times and if it turns out not to be right for you, nothing happens. Pivot. In eCommerce a high-demand product won't remain that way forever, the trick as demand slows, is to anticipate the next trend and pivot into selling that. **Pivoting is entrepreneurial.**

Finally, you don't need to be a millionaire, an influencer or an entrepreneur to earn a comfortable living. You do need to be entrepreneurial. The question is when do you start? If we spend the first half of our lives saying we're too young to start something and the second half saying we're too old, then when?

I hope you've taken a step towards mastering one thing as a result of reading this book.

If you would like to join a mailing list to receive our newsletter or find out more about our work, please visit www.cosmikos.com or email me at fiona@cosmikos.com. You can also sign up for coaching on the website.

Follow us on:
https://www.facebook.com/Cosmikos/

https://www.instagram.com/_cosmikos/

https://www.pinterest.co.uk/cosmikos/

https://twitter.com/fiona_cosmikos

Wishing you every success.

Fiona

What Now?

- Choose one area. It's not about getting the perfect match or the perfect job first time round. Ask yourself what you can become best at in a growth area now. Aim to learn as much as possible about it. Having a goal brings structure and hard work to your day both of which contribute to mental wellbeing.

- Forget multi-tasking. Focus on one opportunity to move you towards earning a living and financial freedom.

- Network for all your worth. Connect to people via apps like Fledglink, on sites like Multiverse, Not Going to Uni, Amazing Apprenticeships or via your student rep at University. Use the communities that are all fired up to support you through this. Connecting to people is important for psychological health.

- Start today. We're constantly reading about how risky it is to do X or Y, but no-one talks to us about the risk of doing nothing.

- Carve rock-solid habits into your day, especially for the first hour. Drink a glass of water, shower, exercise or meditate before checking your phone or making your To Do list.

- Check things off the list. Work in twenty-five-minute stints and aim to achieve something within that time. Have a break and start again.

- Don't fall down the rabbit-hole of watching YouTube for five minutes then three hours later wonder where the time has gone.

- Increase your energy and mental wellbeing by including downtime at the end of your day whether it's playing the guitar or watching YouTube!
- Invest in learning.